8-32

# SO
# THAT'S WHAT
# MISSIONS
# IS ALL ABOUT

# SO
# THAT'S WHAT
# MISSIONS
# IS ALL ABOUT

## WADE T. COGGINS

moody press
chicago

# CONTENTS

# INTRODUCTION

THIS BOOK is intended to be a study guide for groups who want to learn more about current developments in missionary endeavor. Group participation is essential to receiving full benefit from these studies. To assist those with limited experience in teaching through group participation, questions provided at the end of the chapters will stimulate class discussion.

The leader should insist that participants study the material at home. He should reinforce this concept by using class time not to read the material but to secure group participation.

A variety of approaches should be used during the course to maintain individual interest and involvement. Projects should be assigned from time to time. Use the questions in the book and add other assignments of your own. By using a variety of methods you will keep participation alive and vital. At times you may ask a class member to work on a specific question during the week and report to the whole class when it meets. If the class consists of nine or more, the leader should consider the occasional use of "buzz" groups. Accomplish this by asking groups of three or four to study different questions for a short span (five to eight minutes) during class time and then report back to the whole class. The leader can briefly sit with each buzz group to determine that it is functioning.

Before the course ever starts, the leader should check with the librarian to see what books and materials are available. During the course, make assignments that will assure use of the materials. If you need background materials for the course, contact the appropriate church or Sunday school officers to secure them. The bibliography in the back of this book will suggest a number of books which would make good reference materials. As the course begins, glance over all the discussion questions to anticipate long-range assignments that should be made.

The group leader is encouraged to prepare his own questions that relate to the scripture verses and their application to the subject of the discussion.

The aim of this book is to acquaint readers with major currents of contemporary missionary endeavors. It is a widely held misconception that missions is a dying enterprise. On the contrary, missionary work is an exciting movement into which many new methods and techniques are being incorporated to accomplish the long-standing goal to evangelize the world. The insights of many disciplines are being brought to bear on missions, giving new depth to its thrust. New partners are coming into the work as Third World missions are established, making it more truly international and universal. The author's desire is that this study provide new insights and spark new interest which will lead many into greater participation in God's worldwide outreach.

# 1

# MOTIVATION AND GOALS OF MISSIONS

AT THE HEART of all serious thought about missionary endeavor are two questions: Why should we do missionary work? What should missionary work accomplish? Each question is simple, yet complex.

*Motivation.* Most missionaries will testify that they have gone into new areas of the world in response to the command of Jesus Christ, who is their Lord. He commanded. Out of love and commitment to His lordship they went. Many loving disciples need no further explanation or motivation.

Probing further, it is possible to say that missionary motivation is based in the love of God, who took the initiative in seeking fellowship with man and provided salvation through the sacrificial work of Christ on the cross and through the power of His resurrection.

Some modern writers speak of motivation in far different terms. They call upon Christians to take their agenda from the world. They exhort them to look at the *revolution* taking place in the world, and to support it, confident that the revolution is God's work. A book, *Christians in the Technical and*

*Social Revolutions of Our Times,* reports on the World Conference on Church and Society, Geneva, 1966. The book consistently calls on Christians to support world revolution, including violence, as their missionary involvement. Dr. Richard Shaull is quoted as saying, "Christian existence is revolutionary existence, and that the Church's service to the world is that of being the 'pioneer of every social reform,' *without making any claims for Christianity* or trying to Christianize the revolution."[1] Shaull further said, "the temptation of the oppressed to rely on violence should be reduced. But we *would not* go so far as Professors Wendland and Andre Philip to urge exclusive *reliance on nonviolent action or insist that Christians have no participation* in the use of revolutionary violence."[2]

For such "prophets," the missionary endeavor of today is to join the revolution that is bringing turmoil to the world, and to do so without making any claims for Christianity. One method of implementation of this philosophy is the sending of aid to rebel groups in Africa.[3]

Reacting to the widespread influence of the teaching that the Christian is to get his agenda from the world rather than the Bible, a number of German theologians, meeting March 4, 1970, prepared the Frankfurt Declaration to reply to the "insidious falsification of their motives and goals."

> We recognize and declare: Christian mission discovers its foundation, goals, tasks, and the content of its proclamation solely in the commission of the resurrected Lord Jesus Christ and his saving acts as they are reported by the witness of the apostles and early Christianity in the New Testament. Mission is grounded in the nature of the Gospel. . . . We therefore oppose the current tendency to determine the nature and task of mission by socio-political analyses of our time and from the demands of the non-Christian world. . . . According to the apostolic witness, the Gospel is normative and given once for all.[4]

Speaking of a study document prepared for the Uppsala meeting of the World Council of Churches (July, 1968), Donald McGavran wrote:

> Section II has not been thrown together hurriedly or by accident. During the last twenty years, a new theology has been forged which apparently intends to have no place for mission from the Church in one land to Non-Christians in other lands. It intends to divert the whole missionary movement into the movement toward Christian unity on the one hand and Christian behaviour toward one's close neighbors on the other.[5]
>
> Again and again this Draft insists that the Church must be concerned with the World's Agenda. Indeed one heading is The World's Agenda—Our Business. In plain English this means that the mission of the Church is to meet needs of which the world is conscious. Since it is not keenly conscious of the need to believe on Jesus Christ, proclaiming the Gospel should be dropped from the tasks of the Church. This is not said, mind you; but it is a legitimate deduction for everything else is stressed and proclamation of the Gospel is not even mentioned.[6]

The Christian today, confronted by these ideas, should sort out carefully his motivation for giving to missions and for going overseas. He must ascertain conviction and reality which will stand the test of adverse, trying times, and the onslaught of human ideologies.

Motivation is properly anchored in unchanging causes which will not be undermined by the fickle tides of history.

The love of God is an eternal cause which is the crucial element in any true missionary motivation. From God's love emanates His redemptive solution for man's need. It is also that divine love in a Christian's heart which moves him to share Christ with others.

By its very nature, the Church is missionary. Knowing this, every Christian should seek to make his church *mis-*

*sionary* by his personal involvement and participation. The church that is not missionary falls short of its New Testament expectation.

Another unfailing motivating force is a Christian's loving obedience to the authoritative command of Christ as revealed in Scripture. These are among the strands which constitute a solid motivation which can withstand the ravage of time and adverse circumstances. These and other factors blend together in the experience of a dedicated Christian to produce a personal sense of urgency to be involved in God's outreach to the world. Paul spoke of it saying "Woe is me if I do not preach the gospel" (1 Co 9:16). This becomes a personal mandate to reach out in love to those who need the life-giving message of love and reconciliation.

*Goals.* In addition to the question of motivation, the matter of *goals* must be considered. What is missionary work to accomplish once it has been undertaken? Many highly motivated people fail to have a clear goal for their work. A broad goal certainly is to proclaim the salvation of Christ in a meaningful way to every person on earth. This includes the objective to men and women who embrace the gospel in repentance transformed by the Holy Spirit.

> The primary visible task of mission is to call out the Messianic, saved community from among all people. Mission proclamation should lead everywhere to the establishment of the Church of Jesus Christ, which exhibits a new, defined reality as salt and light in its social environment.[7]

Speaking at Urbana '70 on Evangelical Social Concerns, Samuel Escobar, an evangelical leader in Latin America, speaks of the nature of our message when he says:

> Renewal from the Word will teach us to preach again about sin with the precision, acuteness and courage of the prophets who pointed to sin expressed in social injustice and abuse. They pointed to sin where it was, even at the risk of being considered agitators, and were thus faithful to the whole

counsel of God. It is at this point that the faithful preacher becomes a concerned critic of his society of all social classes.[8]

British evangelicals viewing the debate prepared a statement which declared:

> There can be no vital urge to evangelism apart from total commitment to the evangel as the divinely given message of reconciliation between God and man. This involves more than mental assent to the message and the obligation. It means whole-hearted response to the love of God in Christ, and personal commitment to the Saviour Himself, carrying with it readiness to serve Him unreservedly.[9]

The well-known evangelical magazine *Christianity Today* commented editorially on what it called "the Missionary Retreat." After demonstrating a decline of about one-third in missionary personnel from 1958 to 1971 among the larger denominational boards, the reason for the decline was discussed:

> The missionary decline in these old, mainline denominations was preceded by a change of orientation in the ecclesiastical hierarchies. These were the churches that began to turn away from evangelism and personal soul-winning as they came to envision the mission of the church to be changing the world's social and economic structures.[10]

An overriding goal is to publish the Good News that salvation is available to all. The Church desires to give the people of the world an opportunity to make a meaningful choice concerning Jesus Christ. The goal is to present the message with such genuine love, concern, and service that people will be drawn to embrace salvation and be incorporated into the Church.

Manifesting the love of Jesus is a goal that leads the missionary enterprise into an unlimited variety of service, such as: education, medical work, training, in addition to direct evangelistic efforts. All of these should be integrated into the goal of establishing living, expanding churches.

## Scripture Lesson

"Therefore, we are ambassadors for Christ, as though God were entreating through us; we beg you on behalf of Christ, be reconciled to God" (2 Co 5:20).

"But you shall receive power when the Holy Spirit has come upon you; and you shall be My witnesses both in Jerusalem, and in all Judea and Samaria, and even to the remotest part of the earth" (Ac 1:8).

"And this gospel of the kingdom shall be preached in the whole world for a witness to all the nations, and then the end shall come" (Mt 24:14).

"Simeon has related how God first concerned Himself about taking from among the Gentiles a people for His name" (Ac 15:14).

"Go therefore and make disciples of all the nations, baptizing them in the name of the Father and the Son and the Holy Spirit, teaching them to observe all that I commanded you; and lo, I am with you always, even to the end of the age" (Mt 28:19-20).

## Discussion Questions

1. Think of missionaries you know. What do you think motivated them to enter missionary service? What influences do you think helped lead them into missionary work? What could be done in your church to challenge young people for missions?
2. Think of your personal missionary giving. List factors that influence your giving to missions. Through what channels do you receive challenges which the Holy Spirit can use to motivate your giving? *List them.*
3. Make a list of the motivating factors in missionary endeavor mentioned in the chapter, then add others of your own.
4. When you support missionaries, what do you want them to accomplish in their areas of work? How does their present work contribute to that goal?

5. What do schools, hospitals, clinics, and other such ministries contribute to the overall goal of missions? How can missionaries determine whether these are contributing to their goals?

# 2

# THE SCOPE OF THE MISSIONS
# MOVEMENT TODAY

THOSE WHO ARE MOTIVATED by a literal understanding of the
lost condition of man apart from Christ, and by the command
of Christ to His Church, today carry on an impressive program of outreach around the world. It was not always so in
the Church. After the tremendous thrust of the first century,
missionary activity slowed to a trickle during the centuries
that followed. Even the Reformation produced meager fruit
in missionary expansion. During the 1700s, Count von Zin-
zendorf led the Moravians into a dynamic missionary effort.
Their first missionaries went out in 1732. During the next
150 years they sent out 2,170 to various fields.[1] Apart from
this, very little was done.

William Carey is considered the father of modern missions
in that he alerted the churches of England to the obligation
of witnessing to the rest of the world. The Baptist Missionary
Society was formed in 1792. The following year, Carey left
for India to carry on a remarkable work.[2] Except for tempo-
rary dips (related to two world wars) there has been a general, steady increase in the missionary force since Carey's day.

In 1972 the combined total of Protestant missionaries from

all sending countries serving outside their own nation was an estimated 50,000 to 55,000. Of this world total, 35,070 originated from the United States and Canada.[3] These are generally counted by adults. Husband and wife are counted as missionaries, but children are excluded.

The question naturally arises: Who finances, sends and supervises all these people? Overseas, it is not uncommon to find that people think missionaries are financed by government funds. The fact is that none of them are sent by government funds, but by private donations collected in a wide variety of ways by a multiplicity of agencies. Many of the funds are collected by local congregations and contributed to a sending board or society of the denomination. In other cases the funds are collected by an independent missionary agency directly from the donors. This chapter deals with the missionaries going out from North America, although increasingly Western European countries are sending missionaries and technical aid to other countries.

It is estimated that in 1972, $393 million was collected in North America to support the 35,070 missionaries and their related programs.[4] They were sent out by some 584 agencies,[5] which vary greatly in size and significance. Following are the ten largest:[6]

1. Southern Baptist Convention . . . . . . . . . . . . . .2,507
2. Wycliffe Bible Translators . . . . . . . . . . . . . . . . .1,973
3. Churches of Christ . . . . . . . . . . . . . . . . . . . . . . .1,623
4. Seventh-Day Adventists . . . . . . . . . . . . . . . . . .1,546
5. Youth with a Mission . . . . . . . . . . . . . . . . . . . . .1,009
6. The Evangelical Alliance Mission (TEAM) . .  992
7. Assemblies of God . . . . . . . . . . . . . . . . . . . . . .  967
8. United Methodist Church . . . . . . . . . . . . . . . .  951
9. Sudan Interior Mission . . . . . . . . . . . . . . . . . . .  818
10. Christian and Missionary Alliance . . . . . . . . . .  803

There are six principal associations with which missionary agencies in North America can affiliate. The missions which send about 60 percent of the total missionary force are affiliated with one of the six. The following list shows the number of missionaries sent by missions related to the various associations:[7]

Evangelical Foreign Missions Association,
   National Association of Evangelicals[8] .....7,074
Division of Overseas Ministries, National Council
   of Churches, United States .............6,477
Interdenominational Foreign Mission
   Association[9] .........................6,130
Fellowship of Missions ................... 943
Commission on World Concern,
   Canadian Council of Churches ........... 444
The Associated Missions, International Council
   of Christian Churches ................. 65

These associations are not sending agencies themselves, but are made up of church missionary boards and missionary organizations which individually recruit, finance, and send out missionaries. The associations provide for cooperation in government relations, consultation, and to some extent, publications. They offer a form of self-regulation, providing agreed-upon standards for membership, and requiring annual financial statements.

The various missionary boards and organizations are involved in a remarkably wide variety of activities as they seek to carry out the mandate of Christ. From a sample of missionaries, the *Handbook* sought to determine the specific type of work individuals are doing as they carry on their ministry. The following results are reported:[10]

Education .........................44%
Medicine, public health ...............18%
Field administration ..................13%
Literature, all phases .................. 8%
Broadcasting ........................ 6%

Agriculture, community development .... 4%
All others ......................... 7%

In most areas of the world, these activities are carried on in conjunction with the national church. They are very frequently conducted in connection with an evangelistic effort, either by the church or the missionary himself. Much clinic work, for example, is accompanied by an evangelistic and pastoral ministry. A great deal of evangelistic work is carried on in the mission schools. While evangelism and church planting were not included in the above survey as separate categories, many of the efforts are aimed at those goals.

The list undoubtedly points up a need for an appropriate number of missionaries to be assigned to ministries clearly designed to reach out beyond the existing church.

As governments build hospitals, the number of missionaries involved in hospital work goes down. But there is an increasing ministry in clinic work and public health.

Combining literature and broadcasting, the percentage in media surpasses field administration by just one percentage point. This appears to point to a need for greater effort in the use of the media.

Missionaries still conduct virtually all types of work carried on in the past. A significant number of missionaries still work in primitive situations where they begin with the elementary matter of learning the language, reducing it to writing, and then communicating Christ while serving and teaching. On the other hand, many use highly technical skills required in modern radio, TV, and literature. To use these effectively, skills in marketing and research are needed as well as the technical knowhow. Some teach overseas at the graduate level. Practically all the skills are used to some degree in every aspect of missionary endeavor.

The MARC *Handbook* tabulates in percentages where the North American missionaries serve:[11]

Oceania .............. 3%
Latin America ........34%
Asia ................30%
Africa ..............27%
Europe .............. 6%

All this effort around the world pays off. Churches are established and growing. Ralph Winter comments on that growth:

> Many in the absence of careful calculations took it for granted that Christianity was dying out, that the growth of the Christian Church could not keep up with the world population explosion. However, in 1970 various studies revealed encouraging facts. David Barrett . . . showed that Christianity was clearly outracing the population increase in Africa. Christianity constituted three percent of the population in 1900, twenty-eight percent in 1970, and would constitute forty-six percent by the year 2000, according to his cautious projection.[12]

It is important to note that Barrett uses the word *Christian* in its broadest sense, including all who call themselves "Christian." This would include Catholic, Orthodox, and African indigenous groups led by various "prophets."

The most exhaustive survey of Protestant work in Latin America ever undertaken showed the evangelicals to be increasing at an annual growth rate of 10 percent. It found 4,915,400 communicant members in the Protestant churches. By careful calculation of the information it concluded, "there are at least ten million evangelicals in Latin America—but there may be even fifteen or twenty million."[13]

While the Church is growing, the population of the world is also soaring, having reached 3.8 billion by late 1973. Missionaries will continue to have an important role in reaching the world for Christ; and it is increasingly evident that, in order to complete the work, it will be necessary to effectively involve every Christian around the globe in dynamic witness.

## SCRIPTURE LESSON

"And while they were ministering to the LORD and fasting, the Holy Spirit said, 'Set apart for Me Barnabas and Saul for the work to which I have called them.' Then, when they had fasted and prayed and laid their hands on them, they sent them away" (Ac 13:2-3).

"And they passed through Pisidia and came into Pamphylia. And when they had spoken the word in Perga, they went down to Attalia; and from there they sailed to Antioch, from which they had been commended to the grace of God for the work that they had accomplished. And when they had arrived and gathered the church together, they began to report all things that God had done with them and how He had opened a door of faith to the Gentiles. And they spent a long time with the disciples" (Ac 14:24-28).

## DISCUSSION QUESTIONS

1. List some *similarities* and some *differences* between the missionary journey described in the book of Acts and today's missionary program.
2. List reasons why you think mission boards form associations in which they share membership with similar organizations.
3. Describe the philosophy or stance of the various associations with which you are familiar.
4. How many missionaries have gone out from your church?
5. How many missionaries does your church or denomination support?
6. How much does your church or denomination give toward missions annually, per member? (A large group which is among the top ten in the list in this chapter appealed for funds on the grounds that the average contribution per member was only $2.94 annually.)
7. Discuss reasons why your local church has (or has not) produced missionaries for this worldwide work.

# 3

# COMMUNICATIONS

IN THE NEW TESTAMENT the Gospel was spread by oral communication, either to one or a group. Mass media, as we know them, were not in use and are not discussed in the New Testament. The nearest thing to mass media was public speaking which, indeed, was widely used by the Church leaders in New Testament times.

One significant factor which can be observed gives some insight into their philosophy of communication. The Christians went everywhere communicating the Gospel. They did not limit themselves to the accustomed modes of religious communication, which principally involved synagogues or temples. The Christians went to the villages, to the marketplaces, to schools, and other public places to share the Gospel. Projected into today's world, this would seem to support the idea of using all types of media. A comparison of Paul's messages at Mars Hill and one given in a Jewish synagogue (Ac 13) would also indicate that serious attention was given to the matter of cultural differences. Paul obviously built on the understanding that people had to lead them on to a decision.

The goal of missionary work is to communicate. Communications, therefore, permeate every phase of the work and comprise a part of every activity. All kinds of service and ministry form a web of communications which penetrates far beyond verbal expressions. Loving care and concern, which are demonstrated through various kinds of programs that meet the felt needs of people, can be communication at a very profound level. The Holy Spirit, working in and through committed Christians, is the great Communicator. Communication takes place along the network of personal witness, public speaking, distribution of printed materials, provision of relief goods, medical aid, agricultural guidance, the mass media and countless other activities.

These various aspects of communication are too often isolated from one another, and thus fail to converge at a given time and place to influence the populace in a forceful manner. The more they can be coordinated, the more effective they can become. A very intimate relation between communication efforts and established local churches is crucial in creating the desired impact.

The length of this chapter will not permit exploration of all the vast ramifications of communications. It concentrates primarily on the cultural aspects and on the use of media in missionary work. As a basis for exploring the use of media in Gospel communication, it is necessary to look briefly at the problem of cross-cultural communication. Communicators confronting an unknown culture and language need careful preparation, if real communication is to take place.

Donald N. Larson deals with the problem of making our message understandable to those of another culture when he writes:

> We who are concerned with the development and spread of Christian literature often sense that our message is not getting through. Why? How do we account for the "static" interfering with our readers' comprehension? What special problems arise when authors belong to one cultural tradition

and readers to another? Research in anthropology and linguistics is beginning to yield many important insights into communication problems, and from this perspective we can reasonably hope to find better explanations for them.[1]

The Christian communicator has an understanding of the Gospel and is motivated by his love for Christ to express that understanding to someone else. He desires the recipient to understand it and act upon it. It is possible, however, that the recipient who lives within another culture and has a distinct language will not receive the message intended. We recognize that reality when we do not speak his language at all. The problem is more subtle and sometimes not recognized when we have learned a certain number of words in his language and think he is understanding us. It is very possible that he understands the individual words but does not get the total message at all. Larson describes the situation:

> As the receiver picks up the sender's sounds, or the scrawlings that he makes on a piece of paper, he bases his interpretation not only on the meanings he attributes to the words, but also on the sender's voice quality, his gestures, and his personal appearance. This supplementary information serves to reinforce, or sometimes correct, the interpretation of the message itself. As a result of this reinforcement, the message received is somewhat different from the message sent.[2]

Another factor in communication is called *noise* or *interference*. It is a distraction which interrupts the listener (or receiver) and distorts the message he is receiving. The sender of the message is frequently unaware of the interference and assumes the message is getting through with clarity.

Given these problems, how is the missionary to communicate? This points out that he must diligently learn the language and also that he must learn the cultural patterns. This will enable him to anticipate the thought patterns and distractions of the hearer (or reader) and compensate for them.

Robert Gordon illustrates the problem in an article called "The Silent Language Every Missionary Must Learn."

> According to anthropologist Edward T. Hall, vulgar and rude communication may occur while uttering the most polite apology or simply asking a question, like the American agriculturalist who greatly offended an Arab farmer by asking what crop yield he expected at harvest. Such a question is tantamount to calling a fatalistic Muslim a fool. Anybody in his right mind would never try to predict the harvest. Only God knows the future.[3]

Anyone who has lived for a period of time in another culture can provide illustrations of this problem from his own experience. The reality and extent of this problem make it urgent for communicators to be extremely sensitive to the culture in which they serve.

A radio preacher in Latin America, Paul Finkenbinder, is a North American who grew up in Latin America and knows Spanish as well as his own tongue. In the beginning of his radio ministry, he had a program called "La Voz Evangelica" (The Evangelical Voice). In the early years, using a distinctly Protestant name for the program, Finkenbinder reports that only 2 or 3 percent of his correspondence came from unsaved people. The program is now called "Un Mensaje a la Conciencia" (A Message to the Conscience) and is not identified specifically as being evangelical. After the change, correspondence from unsaved jumped to 48 percent of the total. Finkenbinder feels that many never heard the message of the earlier program because there was static or interference caused by the prejudice of the hearer against evangelicals. They turned him off, either literally or figuratively. Finkenbinder says:

> There are millions . . . who are genuinely hungry for God and want the message of Christ (and by the way, I have never watered down, in any way whatsoever, the pure Biblical concept of redemption, justification and holiness of life).

However, these people need to be able to listen to the gospel long enough, to become hungry enough, to realize that a religion, any religion, does not supply that need. They will then seek to be fed with the truth, Christ Himself. For the majority of these listeners, any mention made of a Protestant Church will force them to immediately turn off the program, and we have lost the very thing we want to gain.[4]

In every part of the world there are cultural distinctives like this, and others of greater magnitude, which need to be understood in order to get our message through to the listener. Missionaries have not always had a full understanding of modern cultural insights, but they have nonetheless made extensive use of the media.

Before the era of radio and TV, many lives were invested in learning languages and in the preparation of printed materials to spread the Gospel. It is impossible to calculate the vast number of people who have come to Christ through the printed page. The printed media have been used even more extensively to strengthen Christians and help them grow.

With the exploding literacy rate in the world, the printed page is a greater challenge to the Church than ever before. Modern facilities and techniques make production much more effective. Unfortunately, much of the literary effort of Christians still fails to break through to the masses of the world who do not know Christ as Saviour. Greatly intensified efforts need to be made to provide literature which will attract unbelievers. Channels of distribution which will get it into their hands must be developed.

In a recent experiment, a Christian publisher has prepared an attractive book with a contemporary title and placed it in virtually every secular book distribution point in a small country. A nationwide advertising campaign announced its availability on TV and through newspaper ads. By the end of the second week of the advertising campaign, five thousand copies had been sold. That is more than many evangelical Spanish titles ever sell.

With the coming of the electronic media, missions were quick to utilize radio, recordings, and to some extent the motion picture. Radio outreach overseas was pioneered by radio station HCJB, Quito, Ecuador, in the early 1930s. Some 65 missionary groups are now in broadcasting work, spreading the Gospel around the world. Various approaches are used, each with its own strengths and weaknesses. Great, powerful stations send the message great distances in many languages, usually on shortwave bands. (There are some very powerful stations which use long and medium-wave bands that reach ordinary radio sets.) They reach the people who have the proper receivers to bring in the signal. Mail to such stations indicates that great numbers listen.

Another approach is the small station which is heard in a single language area and is easily picked up on small transistor radios readily available to the populace. In this type of ministry, the programming is usually identified very closely with the people it serves. A Christian station in Haiti uses this approach. It provides practical help for the daily lives of the people, along with Gospel messages. For example, a health program was developed to deal with simple health and hygiene problems. During a two-month period in 1973, a contest was conducted in connection with the program. Fifth and sixth graders were invited to participate in the contest, which offered a prize. The contest generated 22,000 letters. It was evidence of strong local interest in the programs. This type of radio program serves to prepare people and make them receptive.

In the high Andes of Ecuador, a very significant movement of people to the Gospel is taking place. While it is impossible to understand the sovereign workings of God in turning men's hearts to faith, many feel that radio has had a part in preparing the soil. Whatever the reasons, hundreds in Ecuador are turning to Christ.

Some broadcasters strongly recommend the small station, especially for the small language and dialect groups where it is possible to secure permission to build the transmitters. Robert Kellum writes of the opportunities:

> There are some 5,800 language and dialect groups in our world and the Great Commission of our Lord requires ministering His Gospel to each group and person. But every broadcast transmitter has the same limitations, whether it is one hundred or one million watts: it can broadcast only one language or dialect at a time. Therefore missionary broadcasters should consider seriously the present need for hundreds of low and medium power stations to reach the secondary and minor language groups of the world.[5]

Yet another approach to missionary radio is the purchase of time on secular stations. Some very significant things are happening in this field, but there is room for much more development. Paul Finkenbinder's "Un Mensaje a la Conciencia" is carried on more than 250 stations. It is aired 10,000 times each month. In Mexico a concerted effort has placed many programs on secular stations.

In the use of secular television, Evangelist Luis Palau secures time for a live TV program in connection with city-wide campaigns. The program consists of a "hot line" to the evangelist while he is on camera. People call in with their problems, and he has led many to Christ during such live interviews. Alternate numbers, announced for those who cannot reach the studio number, have resulted in many additional interviews with counselors.

James Engel, a well-known authority on marketing research, is now adapting his knowledge and experience in that field to help evangelical communicators. He points out that the potential audience of an evangelical communicator has an extremely wide range of people. It is urgent that the communicator take steps to find out all that he can about the people he desires to reach. Engel points out that all people fall somewhere on a spectrum or continuum ranging from a point of "no effective awareness of the Gospel" to "fully trained discipleship."

| | |
|---|---|
| Sowing | no effective awareness of Gospel |
| | some initial awareness |
| | awareness plus grasp of implications |
| | challenge followed by decision |
| Reaping | decision |
| | immediate follow-up and building |
| Building | initial spiritual growth |
| | growth followed by teaching others (2 Ti 2:2) |
| | fully trained discipleship |

MARKET SEGMENTATION BY SPIRITUAL STATUS

"Everyone will fall somewhere on this continuum. The communication task, then, is to meet people where they are in terms of understanding and move them toward decision and true discipleship."[6]

If the majority of the people in a society or audience segment have only a distorted awareness of Christ, it is likely that they will screen out communication which focuses only on the plan of salvation. The essential content must challenge presuppositions, raise questions, present the Christian alternative. Communication, in turn, will be effective only if it can speak clearly to these issues and move people toward decision.[7]

Engel calls on Christian communicators to make greater efforts to find out what people will read or listen to and radically change the approach to meet them where they are. Borrowing from his past experience in marketing, Engel calls this approach "marketing orientation" which "is initiated with an analysis of the environment, especially the audience. From the information, communication goals are determined, and a program is then designed and is implemented."[8]

When communicators begin to study the target audience and begin to develop a strategy that will get the message through to them, it begins to raise questions which today's communicators need to face. Which media should be used? Realistic planning often indicates that a multimedia approach is needed. Advertisers, for example, use a saturation approach to market a product. They will launch a simultaneous campaign with ads on TV and radio, ads in the newspaper, samples or fliers at the door of every house, representatives in stores with samples, etc.

Some missionary communicators use radio or TV. Some use newspaper ads or print and distribute books. Others go door-to-door with samples (scripture portions)—but when have these ever been coordinated with properly phased timing and a common theme? Increasing interest in audience research should have the side effect of drawing communicators into closer contact. Many of the principal users of the media in Gospel presentation are communicators who are independent of the Church structure and organization. This is especially tragic overseas, where the Church could be a unifying factor in bringing the users of the various media closer together.

A brief mention should be made of an important factor in future communications—the communications satellite. Think of the things you have seen or heard recently which came via satellite. Have you wondered what they may mean to Gospel communications in the near future? It is generally believed that soon, satellites will be capable of broadcasting directly into the homes of the world—a staggering thought. Of it Abe Thiessen writes:

> Happily we recognize radio as a powerful vehicle for the Gospel. Television too is being utilized, though we have much to learn in its proper application. Now the satellite with its worldwide opportunities is before us. Now is the time to prepare young people for specialized positions. Now is the time to plan the strategies, the structures, and the budgets necessary to match the mission entrusted to us.[9]

The early Christians went to where the unconverted people were. Today's unconverted are gathered at many different places, depending upon their culture and development. In many countries they are gathered around the media. Missions work must include effective and coordinated use of the media, yet they must not ignore the person-to-person aspect of communication, which is still absolutely critical in the communication process. This factor must be tied into the use of the media to the greatest extent possible.

Having done all to present the message in a meaningful way, using every possible means, you ultimately find it essential to depend upon the Holy Spirit to communicate in answer to believing prayer.

## SCRIPTURE LESSON

"And Paul and Barnabas spoke out boldly and said, 'It was necessary that the word of God should be spoken to you first; since you repudiate it, and judge yourselves unworthy of eternal life, behold, we are turning to the Gentiles. For thus the LORD has commanded us, "I HAVE PLACED YOU AS A LIGHT FOR THE GENTILES, THAT YOU SHOULD BRING SALVATION TO THE END OF THE EARTH.'" And when the Gentiles heard this, they began rejoicing and glorifying the word of the LORD; and as many as had been appointed to eternal life believed. And the word of the LORD was being spread through the whole region" (Ac 13:46-49).

"And after they had preached the gospel to that city and had made many disciples, they returned to Lystra and to Iconium and to Antioch, strengthening the souls of the disciples, encouraging them to continue in the faith, and saying, 'Through many tribulations we must enter the kingdom of God'" (Ac 14:21-22).

"A wicked messenger falls into adversity, but a faithful envoy brings healing" (Pr 13:17).

### DISCUSSION QUESTIONS

1. What steps can be taken to get more evangelistic books to the non-Christian public? Are there any real evangelical books on the newsstands in your drug stores and supermarkets? If not, why not?
2. If anyone in the class has lived in another language area, let him describe the problems of communicating with the people.
3. Find three basic approaches to radio outreach mentioned in the chapter. List the advantages and disadvantages of each. Which type should be more capable of overcoming cultural distractions? Why?
4. Do you think the broadcasters you hear are doing much to find out what type of format would reach unsaved people? Discuss broadcasts familiar to the class. Have group members make suggestions for a broadcast designed to attract and hold the unsaved.
5. Does your church use any type of mass media in its effort to reach the community?

# 4

# STRATEGIC PLANNING AND RESEARCH

IN EVANGELICAL MISSION CIRCLES there is rising interest in missions planning that involves developing strategy and working toward its implementation. The setting of goals and the evaluation of progress being made toward their accomplishment tends to focus the efforts of a mission and its personnel. By establishing priorities, planning tends to keep efforts centered on reaching the established goal.

A reasonable goal for the Church as a whole is that every person on the earth have an opportunity to understand the Gospel sufficiently to either accept or reject Jesus Christ as his own personal Saviour.

Some immediately question whether planning, research, and evaluation are compatible with the leadership and direction of the Holy Spirit in the work of the Church.

Proponents of adequate planning and research maintain that such planning is indeed an opportunity to allow the Holy Spirit to bring to bear on a given situation all the facts and provide guidance on the best possible approach. The Scripture reflects that God plans ahead. "This *Man*, delivered up by the predetermined plan and foreknowledge of God, you

33

.......d to a cross by the hands of godless men and put *Him* to death" (Ac 2:23).

When the early Church began its day to day work in Acts, the leaders planned goals and made assignments within the overall goals which had been set by the Holy Spirit. Believers were given specific responsibilities that could be measured and checked. For instance, in Acts, chapter six, when the problem arose over the distribution of food to needy believers, the leaders called on the people to choose seven men of whom they said, "whom we may put in charge of this task" (Ac 6:3).

The strategy of the first missionary journey is suggested by the phrase which is used frequently, "they began to proclaim the word of God in the synagogues of the Jews" (Ac 13:5). It was a specific and measurable job to get done. An entirely different emphasis is noted on their return visit.

> And after they had preached the gospel to that city and had made many disciples, they returned to Lystra and to Iconium and to Antioch, strengthening the souls of the disciples, encouraging them to continue in the faith, and saying, Through many tribulations we must enter the kingdom of God (Ac 14:21-22).

Reading the book of Acts with planning and evaluation techniques in mind, it is possible to see repeated evidence of planning by the Church leaders based on facts available and under the leadership of the Holy Spirit.

Ed Dayton calls the failure of Christians to plan a failure to face the future.

> This failure to face the future usually results in a failure to plan for it. There are reasons for this, too. There is the continuing (and creative!) tension between the sovereignty of God (He's going to do it all) and the freedom of man (it's up to me). There are varying views of the mechanisms that God uses to "lead" His people. There is a reaction against "trying to do God's planning for Him."
>
> A failure to plan can also be laid directly at the door of our failure to establish goals, to stick our neck out in faith

and go on record as to what it is we are supposed to accomplish.[1]

As missions leaders become convinced that it is compatible with the leadership of the Holy Spirit to set measurable goals and lay definite plans to accomplish them, the next problem is *how* to plan. Dayton says:

> Planning has to do with goals. This area of goals is really the area where we in the Church have our greatest difficulty. Scientists and business men accuse us Christians of fuzzy thinking because we are fuzzy about our goals. When we in the Church talk about planning, we need to talk about goals, and these goals are accomplishments that must be in terms that are measurable.[2]

Efforts to establish goal-centered planning have brought about the realization that in many places more information is needed to plan effectively. This has established the need for research to assemble the available facts and prepare them in a way that will aid churches and missions in their outreach.

In terms of his work, a missionary's goal may be to evangelize every person in a given geographical area. In order for this to become a *measurable* goal, much information is needed. The population of the area will affect the number of personnel needed to do the job. The language, or languages, spoken within the territory will affect the preparation required. An understanding of the culture of the people will provide guidance on what methods might be effective. Whether they are literate or not will have an effect on the media to be used. How well they are educated will affect the type of personnel needed. These are but a few illustrations of the need for facts when goal-centered planning takes place.

This brings up the question of the value of adequate information in missionary work. Increasingly, missionary statesmen are aware of the role of research in effectively carrying out the Great Commission. Anthropological understanding helps identify those cultural factors which can open the way for the Gospel. Linguistic specialists delve into the secrets of the language to make certain that the message is conveyed in a meaningful way. Sociological studies of the makeup of the social fabric of a group aid in finding the segment of the population that is responsive to the Gospel.

To determine concretely the effectiveness of research as a basis for goal-centered planning, Missions Advanced Research and Communications Center (MARC), a division of World Vision, undertook an in-depth study of Brazil. Done in co-operation with the Missionary Information Bureau in Sao Paulo, Brazil, a 107-page preliminary report was circulated among the churches of Brazil under the title *Continuing Evangelism in Brazil.*

The report contained factual information about the churches in Brazil, including a brief history and current statistical data. It analyzed the population in such matters as growth, density, economic status, and religious life. It related to this the response to the Gospel by the people in various categories and regions. It concluded that the Church in Brazil is in a strong position to evangelize the population at large. Computers were used in the preparation and storage of the data.

In presenting the report to the churches of Brazil for their study and planning the writers said:

> God works in mysterious ways His wonders to perform. He uses all of the technology of each generation to reach that generation and to communicate His love and the saving grace of Jesus Christ. The task of each generation is to understand God's strategy and to take its part in carrying out God's mandate. The more we know about the Church, the people we are to reach, and the milieu in which we find these people, the greater is the probability that we will honor God by carrying out Biblically-based evangelism which meets the cultural need of the day.[3]

> We need to know more about the conversion experience of the Christians who are now there. How has God led them

to Jesus Christ? Studies are now under way to understand
how God has been dealing with the people of Brazil as individuals. This of course relates to methods of evangelism
that is basic information to know. We need to know the role
of literature, radio, personal witness, tracts, and all of the
other things that God uses.[4]

After further research in cooperation with the churches in
Brazil, the completed book, published in 1973 under the
title *Brazil 1980: the Protestant Handbook,* provides an in-
valuable tool for the church leaders in Brazil. It traces the
rapid growth of the Church in Brazil, revealing that out of a
population of approximately 100 million some 3 million are
members of Protestant churches.[5] It goes on to estimate that
eleven percent (about 11 million) call themselves Prot-
estants.[6]

The Brazilian church is being urged to use the data base
now available to project in faith a strategy for providing for
every Brazilian a valid opportunity to say "yes" to Jesus
Christ. To provide help in doing this a Center for Advanced
Studies in Evangelism has been established in Sao Paulo.

The book sums up its challenge to the Brazilian church
saying:

> Sound principles of good planning and effective leadership
> will help to make a contribution in the development of effec-
> tive strategy that will lead to an entirely new enlistment and
> deployment of men and resources in the different phases of
> evangelistic advance that are in motion.[7]

This type of undertaking is sometimes called "diagnostic
research." Facts are gathered with the purpose of evaluating
the health of the Church and to come up with remedies for
its ills. Where extensive studies like the one in Brazil do not
exist, an individual church or denomination can still study its
growth patterns (or lack of growth) and seek to determine
reasons for the findings.

Specific applications of research are being developed in

specialized fields. Adaptations of the techniques of audience or market research are being applied to the use of the mass media in sharing the Gospel with the unbelieving world. Evangelicals experienced in that discipline provide leadership in exploring types of presentations which will reach non-Christians.

James Engel urges users of the mass media to take seriously the matter of understanding the target audiences when he writes:

> Unfortunately, the vast majority of communication efforts are based on the unverified assumption of sufficient audience awareness to permit large scale reaping through the mass media. Missionaries and nationals both freely admit the fallacy of this reasoning, but little, if anything, is available in the language of a given society or audience segment which effectively meets the purposes of pre-evangelism. In other words, it is probable that much communication is improperly targeted and hence falls on unresponsive ears.[8]

The application of information which is gathered through research should lead to establishment of goals and development of strategy.

Commenting on the need for planning, Gordon MacDonald, a United States pastor who has visited many mission fields, stated that

> problems of strategy are frequently at the root of personnel dropouts, sloppy, subpar work, unusual degrees of conflict between field leaders, and field programs that are achieving little if any success.
>
> It is absolutely essential that each field have a strategy statement which covers both its long and short-range plan of attack. Failure to develop such a statement leaves the home board, the director, the supporters, and most of all, the missionaries in doubt as to the objectives of their tasks and use of time.[9]

At the individual level, the missionary's goals may be outlined in a job description outlining what his work is and how it relates to the work of others. MacDonald feels that job descriptions, standards of performance, and periodic appraisals and reviews constitute a "major aspect of missions administration that has not been explored to a reasonable extent."[10]

Increasing interest is being shown in these matters. In September, 1970, about 50 leaders of missions serving in Latin America met for a consultation at Elburn, Illinois. Some of the recommendations related to research and planning:

> We recommend that missions and national churches appoint statisticians with the responsibility of compiling and publishing uniform statistics on church growth and related matters. . . . We recommend that in cooperation with our national brethren specific and measurable goals, both short range and long range, be established for the work, and that these be reviewed and updated periodically.[11]

This finding is representative of a growing interest in the careful use of planning and research. It is coupled (as it must always be) with a serious awareness that while good stewardship is manifest in human effort, true fruition of spiritual labor comes as God intervenes and accomplishes His eternal purposes. Prayer must continue to be the key factor in effective evangelism around the world.

## Scripture Lesson

"Men of Israel, listen to these words: Jesus the Nazarene, a man attested to you by God with miracles and wonders and signs which God performed through Him in your midst, just as you yourselves know—this *Man*, delivered up by the predetermined plan and foreknowledge of God, you nailed to a cross by the hands of godless men and put Him to death. And God raised Him up again, putting an end to the agony of death, since it was impossible for Him to be held in its power" (Ac 2:22-24).

"He who gives an answer before he hears, it is folly and shame to him. The spirit of a man can endure his sickness, but a broken spirit who can bear? The mind of the prudent acquires knowledge, and the ear of the wise seeks knowledge" (Pr 18:13-15).

"Every prudent man acts with knowledge, but a fool displays folly. A wicked messenger falls into adversity, but a faithful envoy *brings* healing. Desire realized is sweet to the soul, but it is an abomination to fools to depart from evil" (Pr 13:16-17, 19).

"He whose ear listens to the life-giving reproof will dwell among the wise. He who neglects discipline despises himself, but he who listens to reproof acquires understanding" (Pr 15:31-32).

## Discussion Questions

1. What should be the ultimate goal of every missionary agency? What activities of the missions which you support help accomplish that goal?
2. Have the class play the role of a board of directors of a mission. Approach the problem of planning to enter a mission field (supposed or real). List some of the things you would want to know about the area under consideration. Where would you go for the information? Outline the objectives of the mission during the first year.
3. List ways in which social sciences (such as anthropology, sociology, and linguistics) are used to improve missionary work.
4. Discuss ways in which audience research can help writers and program producers to communicate the Gospel more effectively.
5. In the chapter we mentioned the goal of the first missionary journey (see Ac 13:5). Discuss the goal of Paul and Silas as they set out on the second journey (Ac 15:40-41).

# 5

## CHURCH GROWTH

THE SUBJECT OF "CHURCH GROWTH," discussed in articles, lectures, seminars, and books, is readily found among major missionary treatises of today. What is Church growth, and why is it important to the Church today? Precise definition is difficult, but a description of some of its characteristics will be helpful.

Church growth theory operates on the premise that the purpose of the Church is to grow and expand by winning converts and adding new members to existing churches, and by establishing new churches. All its ministries and activities should serve to accomplish this goal. Viewed from this perspective, Chuch growth is an *attitude* or philosophy of Christian witness and Church outreach.

God the Holy Spirit is recognized as the vital dynamic of a growing Church. He is seen as working through a variety of factors. Methods which He has honored in one place should be studied to see what principles may be applied to new situations.

The Church growth attitude challenges every churchman and missionary to constantly ask himself how his work for rd is helping the Church to grow by gaining converts and adding new members or by expanding the number of churches. It is a reminder to all against rationalizing slow growth and no growth and accepting it without careful evaluation.

Donald McGavran has doubtless done more to confront our generation with the dynamic of Church growth than any other man. A former missionary to India, McGavran has become the spokesman of this movement that has challenged many to effective missionary work.

He illustrates the need for a Church growth attitude in his book *How Churches Grow:*

> Two younger churches, separated by fifty miles only, and working amongst the same kind of people, often show very different rates of growth. In the same decade one will demonstrate an increase of 250 per cent and the other an increase of 19 per cent. It will never occur to the 19 percenter to shift to the pattern which is currently bringing in 250 per cent a decade fifty miles away. "They have their way of going about things, and we have ours" is more likely to be said.[1]

McGavran shows that a great variety of programs and approaches can be used, but at the heart of them must be "a driving concern of some man or woman that others become disciples of Jesus Christ."

Church growth is also an *emphasis*. It holds that while there are many legitimate activities to be carried on by the Church, all of them should be in proper relationship to the goal of expansion. McGavran once remarked that if you want to know the emphasis of a church or mission, go, not to the manual of policies and principles, but to the annual budget where you will discover the *real* emphasis.

In view of the Church growth emphasis, many missions have begun to carefully evaluate their institutions (medical, educational, agricultural, etc.) to determine their present contributions to the development and growth of the Church. Some institutions have been closed down because they no longer contribute to the goals of the church and mission. In one place, a hospital was closed down, but medical ministries continued in the form of teams who visit rural areas where their work is coupled with aggressive evangelism.

In the context of research, Church growth is a *method* which is approaching enough maturity to be called a science or field of study. A study of statistics makes it clear that in some areas of the world and at certain periods of history the Church grows rapidly; while at other times and places it grows less rapidly and even declines. Church growth seeks to understand the dynamics behind these facts and discover factors which will help those who today invest their lives in the work of the Church to see the desired expansion and growth.

As a science, how does Church growth relate to theology, Church history, missiology, evangelism, sociology, and anthropology? While Church growth is none of these, it draws upon all of them. It proposes to take the knowledge of God, study the facts of Church history, and apply the dynamics of evangelism and missions to reach people within the framework of the insights of sociology and anthropology.

McGavran's elevated concept of growth can be observed in this statement:

> Only those movements which are growing at the rate of 50 percent per decade or more should be considered growing churches. The normal increase by births over deaths is likely to provide a 15 percent enlargement. This leaves a 35 percent increase to be achieved by baptisms from amongst the non-Christian members of that people for the decade as a whole.[2]

McGavran's emphasis can be seen in ten prominent elements of the Church growth point of view, which he outlined for the *Evangelical Missions Quarterly:*

1. God wants Church growth. God wants His lost children found. Church growth is theologically required. It is a test of a church's faithfulness.

2. Finding the lost and bringing them back to the Father's house is a chief and irreplaceable purpose of missions to Africa, Latin America, and Asia, where tremendous numbers are living and dying without Christ. Men also have multitudinous needs of body and mind. The Church is properly engaged in relief of suffering, pushing back the barrier of ignorance, and increasing productivity. But such activities must be carried out in proportion. They must never be substituted for finding the lost.

3. These truths are theoretically accepted by Christian missions and written into their constitutions. Practically, however, both liberals and conservatives—faced with many human needs; often defeated by resistant populations; always bound by previous patterns of action; cumbered by institutionalism in advance of the church; burdened with cultural overhang that leads them to proclaim Christ in Western ways; committed to a non-Biblical individualism; not understanding multi-individual accession as a normal way men come to Christ; and deceived by their own promotional efforts (whatever *our* mission does is wonderful)—constantly underemphasize and betray these truths. Both liberals and conservatives too frequently are content to carry on "splendid missionary work." Bitter experience teaches them to entertain small expectations of church growth, and they spend most of their budgets, time, and missionaries for other things.

4. At this very time, however, the world (a mosaic of peoples) is much more responsive than it has ever been. People after people [are becoming] winnable. Segment after segment can be discipled.

5. Enough discipling is not happening, however, partly because of a lack of knowledge about how to find lost men and build them into the church. This paucity of knowledge can be ended.

6. The hard facts of church increase can be ascertained by research: Where has the church grown? How much has the church grown? Above all, why has each segment of the church grown?

7. These hard facts must be published, taught to missionaries, and read by all serious-minded missionaries.

8. The sciences of man (anthropology, sociology, and psychology) have much to tell us about how men become Christians and make other changes; hence, they should be greatly studied.

9. Church planting evangelism should be greatly increased—by laymen, missionaries, ministers, denominations—along indigenous church lines, by mass evangelism, people movements, personal evangelism, literature, and radio.

10. Theological education should be revamped so that seminaries graduate many men successful in church planting.[3]

Here are a few of the reasons for growth in churches which are getting results. They have been distilled by McGavran in a summary found in *Understanding Church Growth:*

1. Some minister, layman, or missionary dedicated his life to planting churches. 2. The Gospel was preached to some receptive segment of the population. 3. Someone recognized one of many growing points given by God to his church and valuing this beginning poured his life into it. 4. Someone having a particular plan for multiplying churches which fitted his special population, worked and prayed to win people and multiply churches.[4]

McGavran also lists hindrances which he has found in researching churches which do not grow. Some of the reasons he suggests for lack of growth are:

1. Leaders were chained to nonproductive work—possibly once needed, but long outmoded. 2. Church and mission were devoted to an only slightly productive pattern instead of a highly productive one. For example: They continued

the school approach when adults could be won. They baptized no illiterates, though this limited the church largely to youth. They required a three-year catechumenate, though few adults could last the course. They tried to circumvent polygamy by baptizing chiefly unmarried youth and hoping they would stick to monogamy. 3. They did not learn the language of the people, worked always in English, and so established the image that the Christian religion signifies mainly cultural advance. . . . 4. Fearing the problems brought in by converts and churches made up of new Christians, they set very high standards and baptized few. 5. The ministry was too highly trained and paid, was not one with the people, and could not be supported by the churches themselves.[5]

John T. Seamands has said that the practical application of the Church growth approach to missions calls for the following actions:

1. Church and mission administration should be geared to church growth, and organized to multiply churches intelligently and purposefully.
2. Missionaries should be trained in the principles of church growth, and in the sciences of sociology and anthropology.
3. Theological education and missionary orientation should be revamped so that graduates and trainees may be successful in church planting.
4. Missionary personnel and mission finances should be concentrated more on responsive areas and ripened fields, without jeopardizing existing work.
5. There should be constant measurement of church growth and intelligent use of the facts discovered. This will call for careful and uniform record-keeping, widespread surveys with extensive cross-denominational and cross-continental comparisons, the study of historical and environmental factors making for church growth, and serious application of the lessons learned.[6]

Rene Padilla, writing in the *Evangelical Missions Quarter-*

*ly*, has expressed the concern that some feel about the Church growth point of view. He objected to the undue emphasis on numbers which he considers to be inherent in the Church growth approach. This "numerolatry" he charges "has caused an almost complete neglect of theological thinking and has replaced the 'make disciples' with a cheap evangelism." Padilla further claims that "our obsession for numbers has so clouded our vision that we have not given the theological foundation its proper place."[7]

Proponents of the Church growth emphasis seek to avoid the potential danger of becoming too number-conscious, but at the same time strongly urge that good stewardship requires adequate evaluation of the work undertaken by churches.

The Church growth emphasis touches ever-widening circles of evangelical leadership through courses of studies, books, seminars, and workshops. For ten years the Evangelical Foreign Missions Association has sponsored Church Growth Seminars for furloughing missionaries.

They are now spreading overseas. Venezuelan church leaders planned a series of three Church growth workshops to be held at one year intervals, the first of which was held in March, 1972. From the experience of that workshop the need for an instruction book on diagnostic research into Church growth was established.

A book entitled *A Manual for Evangelism/Church Growth* was written by Vergil Gerber, who had been a part of the Venezuelan team. It was translated into Spanish in time for the 1973 workshop and is now being published in several other languages also. In 1972 one group in Venezuela had projected a goal of fourteen new churches during the *three-year* period. After *one* year that group reported that through increased vision growing out of the previous workshop, *nineteen* new churches had been established during the first year.

The advent of a practical *Manual* has accelerated the deployment of teams to hold workshops in various parts of the world to demonstrate to local pastors and leaders how a graph can tell the story of their church's growth or lack of it. The workshops are not designed to be an academic exercise. They are designed to help each leader diagnose the church situation in which he is regularly involved. On the final day they spend time examining their past performance.

At a Church Growth Seminar in Cali, Colombia in September, 1973, five denominations and groups were represented by several leaders of each. At the end of the workshop, each group set goals for the next five years. When these faith projections were combined it revealed that during the next five years they projected a total increase of 140 percent. Some had already projected plans for training and systematic evangelization to accomplish their goals.

Missionary Wayne Weld (Colombia) writes:

> Church growth thinking has found increasing acceptance among missionaries and national leaders as it has been developed and taught in the last decade. But now it is being applied at the grass roots level. As it takes hold of Christians on the growing edge of the Church we can expect to see an explosion in evangelism within the next few years. Church growth workshops in country after country may well be one of the most significant means God uses for the mobilization of the Church in the 1970's.[8]

### Scripture Lesson

"So then, those who had received his word were baptized; and there were added that day about three thousand souls. And they were continually devoting themselves to the apostles' teaching and to fellowship, to the breaking of bread and to prayer (Ac 2:41-42).

"And having favor with all the people. And the Lord was adding to their number day by day those who were being saved" (Ac 2:47).

"But many of those who had heard the message believed; and the number of the men came to be about five thousand" (Ac 4:4).

"So the church throughout all Judea and Galilee and Samaria enjoyed peace, being built up; and, going on in the fear of the LORD and in the comfort of the Holy Spirit, it continued to increase" (Ac 9:31).

"So then you are no longer strangers and aliens, but you are fellow-citizens with the saints, and are of God's household, having been built upon the foundation of the apostles and prophets, Christ Jesus Himself being the chief cornerstone, in whom the whole building, being fitted together is growing into a holy temple in the LORD; in whom you also are being built together into a dwelling of God in the Spirit" (Eph 2:19-22).

## DISCUSSION QUESTIONS

1. Do you know whether the missionaries of your acquaintance are involved primarily in church planting?
2. Do you think the term *fraternal worker* (that is sometimes used to identify missionaries) suggests being involved in church planting?
3. Do hospitals and schools conducted by missionaries of your acquaintance contribute significantly to Church growth? If not, what other valid purpose do they serve?
4. Look back at the practical applications of the Church growth emphasis suggested by this chapter. Go through them one by one and discuss whether missionary boards and missionary training schools with which you are familiar are fulfilling these.
5. What Church growth principles are applicable to your local church situation? (Consider securing a copy of *A Manual for Evangelism/Church Growth* and graphing a growth chart of your church.)

# 6

## SATURATION EVANGELISM

AN IMPORTANT EVANGELISM MOVEMENT seen in many parts of the world today is called by a variety of names. It is often referred to as *in-depth evangelism, saturation evangelism,* or *mobilization evangelism.* Specific manifestations of it have been variously known as Evangelism-in-Depth (Latin America), New Life for All (Nigeria and other countries), Christ for All (Zaire), National Evangelistic Campaign (Korea), Mobilization Evangelism (Japan), Christ the Only Way Movement (Philippines).

No single term has been universally accepted as the proper generic name of this dynamic movement. When viewed from the point of view of scope, saturation is helpful. Its goal is to saturate an area with the witness of Christ. As a method it can well be called mobilization evangelism since it functions well only as believers are effectively mobilized. Its purpose can be thought of as in depth since it seeks to reach all strata of society.

The earliest form to be publicized and receive rather wide attention by evangelicals was Evangelism-in-Depth (EID), developed and named by the late Dr. Kenneth Strachan, then general director of the Latin America Mission. The proposition (sometimes called the Strachan theorum) upon which the movement is projected is "growth of any movement is in direct proportion to the ability of that movement to mobilize its total membership in the constant propagation of its beliefs."[1]

In expanding the description of Evangelism-in-Depth at a gathering of leaders of saturation evangelism from around the world,[2] Ruben Lores, director of Evangelism-in-Depth at that time, said:

> The emphasis is on mobilizing Christians. Every Christian becomes an evangelist. While traditional evangelism seeks to multiply the number of listeners, through the mobilization of the church we seek to multiply the number of evangelists by getting into the experience, motivation and service of each believer. Each Christian is trained, motivated, and incorporated into a definite program of witness.[3]

An Evangelism-in-Depth campaign was first carried out in the Central American country of Nicaragua in 1960. Subsequent campaigns have been carried out in other Central and South American countries. Characteristically set up for a whole country, their goal is an effective witness to every person in the country during a calendar year. The twelve-month schedule usually outlines the following activities in this sequence, with some overlapping: organize committees, start prayer cells, train leadership, train every Christian, carry out visitation programs, conduct local campaigns, conduct special efforts (among men, women, children, youth, minorities, etc.), conduct regional campaigns, a national campaign, and followup.

In Africa a similar burden molded the life of missionary Gerald Swank (Sudan Interior Mission, Nigeria) and prepared him to initiate and lead "New Life for All" in Nigeria. In 1963 he described his vision to a meeting of key leaders:

> Our plan for this programme must not be complicated. It must be simply the evangelism of Nigeria through the mo-

bilization of the church. Neither is it to be merely an increase in missionary activity. It is *all of us together*. Using the potential we already have in the church, we must go out with a simple programme in which in a specific area and in a limited period of time, every man, woman and child shall hear the gospel and understand it.[4]

New Life for All (NLFA) approached the matter a little differently than EID in Latin America. NLFA worked by regions rather than take the whole country at once. The effort was not necessarily limited to a calendar year and the program included about the same special activities conducted by EID programs in Latin America.

Preparation for the visitation aspect in one region in Nigeria was described as follows:

> Long before the instruction classes had finished, the committee on evangelism in each area was already hard at work. Maps of the city and surrounding area were either procured or produced; suburb by suburb, section by section, street by street they were studied. Villages, hamlets, Fulani camps, and even farm dwellings were included. None must be missed; "every creature" was the goal.[5]

Some reports about Evangelism-in-Depth convey some of the excitement in great final days characteristic of the early campaigns.

> On Sunday morning, November 21 (1965), fifteen thousand evangelicals in La Paz [Bolivia] took their witness to the streets. It was an impressive sight. It took them two hours and twenty minutes to stream past a single point along the parade route.[6]
>
> I stood on a truck and watched them march past. After the motorcycle escort came the national committee of Evangelism-in-Depth, followed by the uniformed choir. Next marched the university students and what seemed an endless succession of well-dressed businessmen, ragged farmers and tiny school children. Most colorful were the Indian women, their babies slung across their backs in brightly colored

shawls, their brown felt derbies planted securely above their Indian faces. Equally impressive were the tin miners with helmets and goggles, the typical peasant bands, and the colorful floats.[7]

After extensive, on-the-spot research in Latin America, Asia, and Africa, Dr. George Peters, professor of World Missions at Dallas Theological Seminary, concludes that, "A new age of evangelism has broken in upon the evangelical wing of the Church of Jesus Christ."[8]

These movements have aided the churches in areas where they have taken place. Massive training programs among believers provide new leaders for local churches after the campaign is over. Prayer cells, organized by the thousands during the saturation efforts, encouraged believers in prayer and in many cases became evangelistic groups. With all of the positive results of these movements, there still remains the question of the relative growth of the churches where these campaigns have taken place. The movements in Africa are too new to produce substantial statistics for study.

Peters reports the following figures in his study of Evangelism-in-Depth as the number of professions of faith reported for the year:[9]

| | | |
|---|---|---|
| Nicaragua | (1960) | 2,604 |
| Guatemala | (1962) | 20,000 |
| Bolivia | (1965) | 19,212 |
| Peru | (1967) | 25,000 |
| Costa Rica | (1961) | 3,153 |
| Venezuela | (1964) | 17,791 |
| Dominican Republic | (1965) | 11,800 |
| Colombia | (1968) | 22,000 |

After making this study of the statistics for these eight countries for the year of the Evangelism-in-Depth campaign, Peters researched church growth during a ten-year period surrounding the year of special effort. He was seeking to answer the question, "Does Evangelism-in-Depth enlarge and multiply churches?"

> A comparative study of the statistics available indicates that the professions the year preceding Evangelism-in-Depth ranged from sixty-five to seventy-eight percent of the records of the Evangelism-in-Depth year. It is safe to assume that an average seventy-two percent professions would have been made without Evangelism-in-Depth efforts, or that approximately twenty-eight percent of the above figures are the result of the Evangelism-in-Depth program. In several cases the years following the Evangelism-in-Depth thrust, professions and accessions were lagging behind the years preceding the program, indicating that the biological supply of converts and sympathizers of the evangelicals had been pushed forward by a year or two because of the intensive drive of the Evangelism-in-Depth year.[10]
>
> This seemingly affected from three to five percent. Accepting four as the average, we need to reduce the twenty-eight percent by this number. This leaves us with twenty-four percent net gain.[11]

Peters calls this increase in professions of faith a "creditable, healthy and strong" showing for the program. In pursuing the question of growth of church membership Peters finds that we are "confronted by the baffling fact that a comparable rise in figures cannot be shown in church membership."[12]

An "ill-prepared" church, which fails to follow through with those who make professions, is a major cause for the sparse church growth resulting from the saturation movement. Peters suggests that in future campaigns saturation evangelism needs to be designed to "build evangelism effectively and enduringly into the life of the churches." The program ought to "sell the idea of conducting a one-year training program, assisting the churches to reform and mobilize themselves to move ahead aggressively, cooperatively and coordinately to complete the job, either in a continued united effort or a prolonged coordinated movement."[13]

Dealing with the question of retaining for church growth those who make professions of faith, Edward F. Murphy urges greater efforts to provide for such retention in the planning of saturation evangelism.

> If it is strategic to help the churches increase their seed sowing it is even more strategic to help them increase their harvesting. Seed sowing alone is really little more than the beginning stage in evangelism. *The goal of saturation evangelism must be the multiplication of new believers and the multiplication of new churches. We must restructure our programs in the light of this goal even if it means neglecting some other aspect of our strategy.*[14]
>
> The Last Months of the Evangelism Program should be Dedicated Exclusively to Follow Through Evangelism.
>
> Too often these months are dedicated to the grand climax of the seed sowing ministries, the united crusades and evangelical parades. This is a mistake. The follow through program should not be crowded aside in favor of these more spectacular events. . . .
>
> The leaders of the saturation evangelism movement are responsible to see to it that the greatest emphasis is given to follow through evangelism during the last months of the program.[15]

The leadership of saturation evangelism efforts around the world are seeking to enlarge and enhance the ministries of the churches. Evaluation and reevaluation through research and study serve to improve the programs. The programs seek to meet increasingly the needs of those who are contacted through campaigns. During a typical year of saturation evangelism, literacy teams teach thousands of illiterate adults to read. In Bolivia, about thirty Goodwill Caravans took the services of doctors, dentists, nurses, agronomists, and literacy experts to remote and underprivileged areas of the country.

Gerald Swank, founder of the New Life for All program in Nigeria, feels:

there is a recurring need for the full saturation evangelism program at least every five years, perhaps oftener in some places. The impetus that this gives to the program of the local church is very great. The impact is also felt in every part of the nation. New believers become involved in this tremendous experience for the first time.[16]

As the kernel idea of saturation evangelism has spread around the world, it has been adapted to local situations and revised as research and consultation pinpoint weaknesses in the early campaigns.

A major component of the effort called "Christ the Only Way" in the Philippines has been the development of thousands of lay study groups formed in the homes of believers. The hosts of the study groups are a natural bridge to the churches which they attend, and newly evangelized people find their way into the churches. New congregations also spring up through the groups.

A saturation evangelism program in Vietnam, known as "Evangelism Deep and Wide," from the very beginning set the goal to establish churches. These churches are to become vital living units which enter into continuous evangelism and extend the effort far beyond the year (or other time segment) of the saturation program. This kind of adaptation moves evangelism concerns closer to the ideal of churches involved in continuous evangelism.

The inspiration and challenge of the Evangelism-in-Depth campaigns in Latin America doubtless worked in concert with many other currents of evangelism to move vast numbers of believers around the world into greater efforts in outreach.

## Scripture Lesson

"And Saul was in hearty agreement with putting him to death. And on that day a great persecution arose against the church in Jerusalem; and they were all scattered throughout the regions of Judea and Samaria, except the apostles. And some devout men buried Stephen, and made loud lamentation over him. But Saul began ravaging the church, entering house after house; and dragging off men and women, he would put them in prison. Therefore, those who had been scattered went about preaching the word. And Philip went down to the city of Samaria and began proclaiming Christ to them" (Ac 8:1-5).

"And thus I aspired to preach the gospel, not where Christ was *already* named, that I might not build upon another man's foundation; but as it is written, 'They who had no news of Him shall see, and they who have not heard shall understand' " (Ro 15:20-21).

"You did not choose Me, but I chose you, and appointed you, that you should go and bear fruit, and *that* your fruit should remain; that whatever you ask of the Father in My name, He may give to you" (Jn 15:16).

## Discussion Questions

1. Re-read the "Strachan theorum" and discuss its implications (a) for missionaries, (b) for your own local church.
2. One goal of cooperative saturation evangelism is to give a testimony of oneness in Christ without compromising the faith.
   *a*) Can this goal be accomplished by asking participating groups to sign a statement of faith?
   *b*) Can it be accomplished by having a select committee choose the leadership of the cooperative evangelistic campaign?
   *c*) Would it be advisable to allow anyone who is interested join the program regardless of where he stands?
3. If a cooperative saturation evangelism effort were organized in your city or county, on what basis would your church cooperate? Would it be necessary to restrict the pastors who might cooperate? On what basis? Would the same safeguards (or lack of them) be appropriate overseas in the missionary situation?

4. In most year-long programs of evangelism in Latin American countries the year has culminated in large national campaigns in the capital city drawing evangelicals and sympathizers from many churches and from many parts of the country.

   *a*) Do you think this would aid in, or distract from, ultimate involvement in the local church by the new converts?

   *b*) Do you have any alternate suggestion on the timing of such an event?

# 7

# THEOLOGICAL EDUCATION BY EXTENSION

THE RAPID GROWTH of the church in Latin America, Africa, and parts of Asia has created a crisis in leadership. The need for trained workers to lead the multiplying churches reached such magnitude in some localities that leaders began to seek a radical solution.

In many places the vacuum is filled heroically by local leaders who guide the churches as elders or deacons. In reality, they are functional pastors of the flock. These men, however, frequently have only marginal formal education of any kind and no theological training.

The European and North American pattern of training young men in urban seminaries and placing them as pastors of primitive churches has been copied in most mission areas. In many cases the results have been less than satisfactory. Too often the young men, after several years in the Bible institute or seminary administrated by foreign missionaries, become separated culturally from the people they grew up with. Upon returning they may not be accepted as leaders, even though they have the formal training. In many cases the men themselves no longer feel at home in their communities. Additionally, they find it difficult to live on the money and goods the people in the congregation can provide.

Such a situation increases the temptation for the young trainee to gravitate to the city where his talent and ability are much in demand in the developing commercial community. The attrition from the ranks of theologically trained young people became dramatically high. The problem cried for a solution.

Leaders of the Evangelical Presbyterian Seminary of Guatemala decided to develop a new approach to the problem. In addition to having students at the seminary, they arranged to take theological training to the functional leaders of the church. To do this, it was necessary to develop self-teaching materials. Under the plan, professors travel to outposts where they meet with students on a weekly basis. The quality of the training remains high. It is not a correspondence course. The students meet the traveling professor weekly to review their work, to be tested, and to receive new assignments. The weekly meeting place may range from simple to elaborate. In one case the professor met four students under a rural highway bridge.

All the while the student continues with his normal responsibilities. In many instances he is a married man who continues his normal employment to support the family. In addition, as a lay teacher he may be the shepherd of a congregation. To get training under this system he does not abandon these roles. He sets his own pace, choosing to enroll in one, two, or three courses, depending on the time available. It may take a number of years to complete his training, but this is no problem, for at the same time he carries on a fruitful, productive life. His training is immediately put into use, so it is more meaningful to him.

The Guatemala experiment was launched on two assumptions: "(1) that you can find leadership gifts in the specific subcultures of a church, be they Indian, rural Spanish, professional, or some other subculture, and (2) that you can train them where they are."[1]

This concept of education is radically different from the purely institutional approach.

> The extension seminary involves first of all a change in mental attitude for those who have been involved in traditional institutions. If we were to seek a slogan for this change, I would call it "the humanization of theological education."
>
> The extension philosophy involves starting with the *Person* rather than the *institution*. If a given person should be receiving ministerial training, the institution should see that he gets it, according to this new mentality. No possible alternation of the structure of the institution should be discounted which will enable more of God's chosen men to take theological studies.[2]
>
> The calling of the seminary is to train the leaders that God has already made.[3]

In a similar view Peter Savage raises questions about the institution and the student:

> How can we best train the potential or actual leaders at the education level they have already attained? The church demands a multi-level leadership: rural-urban, national-international. How can we so diversify our program to meet this challenge without attempting to steamroll everyone on one simplified stratum? Furthermore, how can we make our programs flexible enough so that the student can study at the pace that he is most capable of, a pace that will draw the best out of him, without forcing him into an impartial and impersonal structure? Could we not reverse our structures? Instead of the student's adjusting to the school, could not the school adjust to the student?[4]

The overwhelming answer by mission leaders around the world is affirmative. Theological institutions large and small are moving to take theological training to the leaders of the

Church. People of all ages are being trained. This concept of training is beginning to operate in the secular educational world also. It is described in *U. S. News and World Report:*

> A new approach to higher education, offering millions of Americans a "second chance" for a college degree, is about to be tested on a large scale. This new kind of education will be offered in experimental institutions called "colleges without walls" . . . People with jobs will be able to take advantage of this type of low cost education without suspending their career in midcourse and without losing income or uprooting families to return to college.[5]

One experiment described in the article is the Empire State College, a new learning center created in New York State. Its first "learning centers" opened in Albany and Rochester in 1971. Thousands inquired about getting into the Empire State program when it was announced to the public. By 1973, centers had been added in Manhattan and Long Island to bring total participants to over 900. From each center satellites form to spread the web farther out.

Many variations of the programs exist and adaptations emerge from the experiments carried out. The variation known as Theological Education by Extension (TEE) has an academic base. While continuing experience is encouraged during the educational process, the program calls for a definite plan of instruction under the supervision of teachers. Though characterized by flexibility which adjusts to the needs of the student, it is academic in nature, with assignments and tests.

The mission field experience, so far, indicates that such a flexible program is desired by the people. In Guatemala, the Evangelical Presbyterian Seminary saw enrollment jump from 7 to over 200 in a period of six years when the extension concept was introduced. While the concept of theological education by extension gains in popularity, church leaders and educators are confronted with the enormous task of preparing adequate self-teaching or programmed texts needed for success of the program. When the student must do the bulk of his studying away from the teacher and on his own, special books are essential.

Producing programmed texts needed for this work is an intricate work that requires special training as well as a thorough knowledge of the academic material, the language, and the culture.

In view of the immense response to the concept around the world and efforts to get the program moving everywhere, Ted Ward of Michigan State University, an eminent leader in the field of programmed materials, warns that

> a glut of poor programmed instruction can spoil the whole business, even if it is done in the name of "getting something started." Now why do I think this? This is exactly what happened in the American public schools. Programmed instruction came on the scene about a dozen years ago. It was seriously oversold. Very poor programs were adopted by school boards. The teacher says, "This is for the birds." They put it on the shelf and didn't even use it. Now you can't even talk about the subject in many school systems because school boards were so badly burned with stuff that they have, still untouched, in great warehouses. Now that could happen to us if we oversell and move too fast and get beyond our quality control.[6]

It is urgent to train in programming skills those who have a knowledge of their subject matter, the language and the culture.

> What we need above all is a procedure whereby we can train people on the field in small groups, two or three at a time in their own school or wherever they serve. . . . We want materials, tapes, films, filmstrips, and programmed instruction in programmed instruction which will teach each of these stages of proficiency and package them.[7]

Seminars to train missionary and national educators in the techniques of writing programmed or self-teaching materials are held in the United States and overseas by teams of experts in the field. This enables a number of writers to produce such texts in the language and culture where they serve. Materials for the TEE projects overseas consist mainly of books that are programmed with questions and instructions to aid the reader's comprehension. In some areas, cassette tapes are also used to a limited degree.

More sophisticated and highly developed teaching hardware, such as TV and TV cassettes, is not expected to find wide application overseas in the immediate future.

As these programs become operational, what will be the application at the local level? Covell and Wagner summarize:

> It is the task of theological education to locate the person to whom God has given these specialized gifts of the ministry, and assist them to develop their gifts to the highest degree possible. The specific objective is to provide them the training that will allow them to meet whatever requirement their church or denomination has established for public recognition as a minister. This is usually called ordination, but not always.
>
> If we base our leadership training on spiritual gifts which have been tried and proven, we will find that the majority of our students are mature men with homes, families, jobs and community responsibilities. This is a description which does not too well fit the typical student whom most of us have been training through the years. It does fit I Timothy 3:1-7.[8]

Considerable impetus was given to the spread of the Theological Education by Extension (TEE) concept by teams who travel to many parts of the world under the sponsorship of the Committee to Assist Missionary Education Overseas (CAMEO, joint committee of IFMA and EFMA). Following seminars in many places, local committees coordinated the production of materials in a country or language group. It has become a movement which is vital in many areas, but not controlled by any central agency.

Statistics prepared by CAMEO in May 1973 resulted in the following statement: "This partial report gives us 814 centers where TEE is used with an enrollment of over 12,300 students. . . . We believe that if a complete report were available there would be approximately 900 centers with 14,000 students."[9]

Proponents of Theological Education by Extension see it as a close ally of Church growth because it will prepare great numbers of leaders to shepherd multiplying churches without uprooting young men and making them financially dependent on the mission or church. Self-supporting ministers adequately trained will augment the possibilities for multiplying churches and providing them with leadership.

## SCRIPTURE LESSON

"You therefore, my son, be strong in the grace that is in Christ Jesus. And the things which you have heard from me in the presence of many witnesses, these entrust to faithful men, who will be able to teach others also" (2 Ti 2:1-2).

"It is a trustworthy statement; if any man aspires to the office of overseer, it is a fine work he desires to do. An overseer, then, must be above reproach, the husband of one wife, temperate, prudent, respectable, hospitable, able to teach" (1 Ti 3:1-2).

"Go therefore and make disciples of all the nations, baptizing them in the name of the Father and the Son and the Holy Spirit, teaching them to observe all that I commanded you; and lo, I am with you always, even to the end of the age" (Mt 28:19-20).

"And God has appointed in the church, first apostles, second prophets, third teachers, then miracles, then gifts of healings, helps, administrations, *various* kinds of tongues" (1 Co 12:28).

## Discussion Questions

1. Do you think the European/American pattern of training the clergy has always been the pattern throughout church history?
2. Do you think the extension seminary concept of training would work in the United States? List the reasons. Discuss any examples with which you are familiar.
3. What is different about the overseas situation? List ways TEE can help overseas churches.
4. How is it possible to determine a person's gifts before his training begins? List ways to identify and develop spiritual gifts among the youth of your church.
5. Describe any self-teaching or programmed materials with which you are familiar (in any subject). If you have a sample available, take it to class.
6. How can TEE promote church growth?

# 8

# MISSION-CHURCH RELATIONSHIPS OVERSEAS

THE SUCCESS of missionary efforts around the world is the basis of what is frequently called a missions "problem." If missions had not succeeded in winning converts and establishing churches, there would be no problem of relating to the national church. The joy of seeing a church form and develop does not change the necessary reality to relate to that church constructively as it matures.

In most countries of the world there is a body of believers who have come to a living faith in Christ. They have, in most cases, trained capable leaders who desire to take positions of leadership. What then is the role of mission?

Three basic options are open to the mission when a church reaches a place of maturity which enables it to manage its affairs reasonably well: (1) the mission may move out lock, stock, and barrel and assume its work has been finished in that country; (2) it can pull out all its people and continue to send funds under some agreed-upon arrangement; (3) it can continue to operate alongside that church and find proper relationships and patterns of structure.

Whatever pattern is worked out, the goal should be to pro-

duce a dynamic which will reach the unevangelized population of that nation with the Gospel. The aim is to find an
arrangement that allows the supporting constituency to carry
out its legitimate missionary function through the mission
without smothering or hindering the true development of the
maturing church. The secret is to find a way to accomplish it.
A further goal should be to help the maturing church to also
become missionary in outlook. It is not a simple matter to
find the proper relationships and structures.

> The unresolved tensions or ill-structured relationships be-
> tween missions and national churches constitute one of the
> most serious obstacles in dynamic evangelism and church
> growth. So, the intermission, interdenominational and inter-
> church relationships are deep underlying causes for much
> failure in missions. Evangelical missions have been strangely
> evasive in this matter. Yet, it is a pressing and urgent cul-
> tural and also spiritual issue upon which much depends in
> the dynamics of missions and church growth.[1]

Many harsh words are being written to make the point
that the day of mission colonialism must end, and the emerg-
ing churches must not be hindered from reaching maturity
and true autonomy. One element that stands in the way is the
19th-century concept of the mission station or mission com-
pound where the missionary lives in isolation from the people
he serves. For this problem Dennis Clark suggests a radical
solution. "One solution to this carryover of the colonial era
would be to dismantle all foreign mission compounds as well
as break up concentrations of foreign personnel having authority over the people who are being served."[2]

A very extreme view was presented by E. P. Nacpil, dean of
Union Theological Seminary, Manila, Philippines, in an article
in the *International Review of Missions*:

> There is one thing he [the missionary] can always count
> on, however; namely, the secure structure, support, and
> efficiency of his board of missions and his right to live the

standards of a developed and superior culture in a developing world in whose desire for liberation he wants to help! Thus, the modern missionary system and its affluent and efficient standards and personnel come to stand alongside the younger churches which are struggling for identity and selfhood. Whom does the missionary serve and what does he do? Is it God or man? Is it the struggling receiving church or the affluent sending church? Is it the local Christian community or the missionary system and its board of mission? Is it the developing society or his own developed society and superior culture?[3]

Nacpil also offers a radical solution. "I believe that the present structure of modern missions is dead. And the first thing we ought to do is to eulogize it and then bury it, no matter how painful and expensive it is to bury the dead."[4]

To replace missions, Nacpil suggests the following:

The work that it entails is to be determined as a necessary and urgent expression of the mission of the inviting church and it must be supported primarily by the faithfulness and stewardship resources of that church. If additional funds are deemed necessary to undergird the work, it will be the responsibility of the inviting church to secure the funds from anywhere and anyone. The missionary will be completely and solely responsible to the church that invites him and in whose life and mission he shares in the same depth and intimacy and freedom as is possible to those who are national participants.[5]

In a far different vein the Sudan Interior Mission describes the process of "nationalization" of missions functions in Nigeria as "an exquisite kind of anguish."[6] The article discloses that the churches related to the Evangelical Churches of West Africa (ECWA)—brought into being by the Sudan Interior Mission—now number some 1,200 local congregations. The national church (ECWA) carries all the expenses of the local churches and supports all her pastors and evangelists. That is the basis of the joy of success. The anguish comes in trying to work out partnership financing for the more complex ministries during the transfer of mission responsibilities to Africans.

The article illustrates the problem. At the Igbaja Seminary (Nigeria) a United States-trained Nigerian has taken over the position of vice principal from a missionary. The missionary's support came from the United States, but the Nigerian's does not. Consequently, the cost of the seminary program went up by that amount.

"Today ELWA (a Christian radio station in Liberia) African staff outnumbers missionary staff two to one. And that is why mission leaders talk about ELWA's success with moans and delight. Unlike some other ministries, ELWA has absolutely no way to produce income."[7]

The subject of mission-church relationships held center stage at the Green Lake (Wisconsin) study conference (GL 71) in October 1971, where over 400 mission executives from missions associated with the Evangelical Foreign Missions Association and the Interdenominational Foreign Mission Association met to lay groundwork for improving relationships.

Many of those gathered at Green Lake acknowledged that some remains of paternalism and colonialism still taint their relationships. Many went away determined to seek better relationships and to build better patterns of structure. In seeking to determine right relationships in any given situation, many factors must be considered. It is necessary to look at the age, history, culture, and other factors which affect the outlook of believers in that church.

A few years ago some denominations developed a pattern of structure called "fusion" or "integration." In this pattern the mission in a given country is absorbed by the national church which it has formed. It may become a department of the national church, which in turn receives the money which comes from the sending countries. It assigns and pays any missionaries that may be requested, and the missionaries function within the church as members.

While it appears ideal on paper, critics of the plan feel that in practice the infusion of foreign money and personnel into the national church structure tends to smother its real initiative and development. In practice it has also tended to cause an identity crisis for the missionary, making it difficult for him to function.

Another pattern is called "dichotomy." Under this structure, the mission continues to exist in the country involved. At the same time the national church operates as an autonomous body with its churches and elected leaders tied together in an association or denomination.

In a typical country the church may be quite mature, yet most of the population of the country has still not been reached with the Gospel. Under an arrangement of dichotomy, the mission will have its own organization which will assign missionaries to a program of outreach. Obviously, unless there is very close liaison, this could lead to problems.

A pattern which has proven efficient for some is called "modified dichotomy." Of this approach Louis King said at GL '71:

> Those who practice modified dichotomy believe the existence of the new churches has without doubt added a new dimension to missionary work—that younger churches do need assistance in certain specialized areas. They therefore propose the mission's resources in personnel and finances be divided. One segment would be (1) for maintaining liaison and vital support with the national church, the other (2) for pioneering and planting by the mission.[8]

Under modified dichotomy, the mission continues to exist alongside the church. The church functions as an autonomous body. There is a joint board or committee made up of leaders of the church and the mission. They meet together to develop strategy, work out agreements on areas of responsibility. Plans are drawn up together. Proponents of this pattern point out that it respects the missionary nature and function of the sending church, and yet preserves the freedom and autonomy of the new church which has developed. As the mission generates new churches through its evangelistic outreach, they become an integral part of the national church. The national church also carries on evangelism which forms churches that are also adopted into the same church body.

King goes on to explain how this relationship is practiced in the actual field situation.

> At the field level where certain ministries of the church and the mission coincide, we have discovered that administrative bridges are helpful. Although both church and mission maintain a legitimate independence of each other, it should not mean they thereby lost contact. Within the scope of administrative dichotomy, there is room and plentiful reason for mutual counseling and talking of ways to expedite the work jointly. This we do through regularly scheduled joint meetings of the executive committees of the mission and the national church. These meetings are essentially for sharing views and formulating plans.[9]

At GL 71, George Peters espoused what he called a pattern of, "mutuality and equality," or "partnership."

> Partnership is not an easy way out of tensions. Tensions are not our foe unless we make them such. Partnership in the true sense of the word is a high ideal—a New Testament ideal—expressing mutuality and equality in the body of Christ. Thus the sending church is neither lording the situation nor is she being lorded over. Rather, the sending church and the national church jointly become the servant of the Lord to a world destitute of salvation and the gospel of God. . . .
>
> Partnership of equality and mutuality is as much an attitude, a relationship, a philosophy, a way of missions as it is a pattern of legislation and administration.[10]

Whatever structure finally evolves in a given situation, it is urgent that the attention of the church and the mission be directed to the unbelieving remainder of the population of the country. In all countries, including the United States, there is enough evangelizing to keep everybody occupied. The challenge is to get some sort of happy relationship built and then move on to the great task of the Church.

## SCRIPTURE LESSON

"And I do not want you to be unaware, brethren, that often I have planned to come to you (and have been prevented thus far) in order that I might obtain some fruit among you also, even as among the rest of the Gentiles" (Ro 1:13).

"And when they had appointed elders for them in every church, having prayed with fasting, they commended them to the LORD in whom they had believed" (Ac 14:23).

"But speaking the truth in love, we are to grow up in all *aspects* into Him, who is the head, *even* Christ, from whom the whole body, being fitted and held together by that which every joint supplies, according to the proper working of each individual part, causes the growth of the body for the building up of itself in love" (Eph 4:15-16).

## DISCUSSION QUESTIONS

1. Diagram on the board the various patterns of mission-church relationships described in the chapter.
   a) Which pattern do you think they use on the fields you have heard about?
   b) Do you have a preference for any plan?
   c) List the weaknesses and strengths of each.
2. List under *church* in the order you think they will be assumed by the national church the following ministries: college, pastorate, high school, tract distribution, hospital, Bible sales, radio station, clinic, printing press, editorial work, primary schools, literacy campaigns, visitation.

3. Situation for discussion. Country A has a population of 25 million. Four percent are believers. Fifteen missions work in the country. "Far Out Mission" has worked there for fifty years. The national church has produced 50,000 believers who worship in 1,000 congregations. The national church is autonomous, and all pastoral work is handled by national leaders. List the possible ministries of the missionaries who remain.

4. Think of the mission fields you have heard about. How large is the national church? What percentage of the population are believers? How many ordained national pastors are there? What types of work are the missionaries doing?

# 9

## WHAT MISSIONS TO SUPPORT

THE GREAT OPPORTUNITIES for evangelization in the world today and the comparative affluence of the evangelical public in the United States and Canada have created a situation where appeals for money have multiplied enormously. Emotional appeals to save "starving children" or "dying souls" bombard the Christian regularly. He must attempt to practice good stewardship in determining where to send his gifts for the best results in God's work.

Good stewardship must first of all be based upon prayer. The leadership of the Holy Spirit operates most effectively in the informed minds where solid facts are available for Him to use in providing guidance. Common sense is in order to determine some things about fund raisers.

Any Chamber of Commerce will tell you that at the fringe of the legitimate business community there are always a few racketeers who prey upon a gullible public with gimmicks and fraudulent deals.

Unfortunately, there are questionable groups who operate as evangelical missions and make appeals and accumulate funds which are used for personal gain. The number is very small. Also, a segment of sincere people make unethical appeals with deceptive advertising. Still others have good goals and motivation, but because of inefficiency in the operation they spend far too much of the income on expenses and advertising.

Confronted with these possibilities, how does the sincere Christian determine where he will send money he wishes to invest in the evangelization of the world? The *Mission Handbook: North American Protestant Ministries Overseas* lists over 600 missionary agencies.[1] It is a complex problem for potential donors to evaluate the appeals for help.

The church situation of the individual will partially determine the exposure he has to missionary appeals. The person whose main church contacts are within a denominational church may have comparatively little exposure to independent agencies. From time to time he gets an appeal in the mail from some agency which has bought a mailing list that includes his name. If his denomination is evangelical and carries on an aggressive missionary program, he will probably give most of his money through his church to the various phases of its missions program.

The contributor who is a member of a denominational church which has a missionary program with which he does not agree, has a different set of problems. He is generally looking for a missionary organization which offers an opportunity to support an aggressive, evangelistic, church-planting ministry. This interest will lead him into contact with a number of independent agencies and various individual missionaries. He must then determine ways to evaluate them and decide which to support.

The contributor in an independent church which has no denominational ties will generally be confronted with the choice of giving missionary money to the church and allowing the missionary committee to decide where to use it, or giving to one or many of the missionary organizations which make appeals through the church, or to him by direct mail.

Not only does the individual's situation influence his missionary giving, but also the type of organization which interests him can vary widely.

The *denominational mission* board or society is typically controlled and operated by the denomination. It is one of numerous agencies supported and managed by the denominational leadership. In many cases the contributor gives his offering and the denominational leaders decide how it will be divided among the agencies. He can influence the use of the money only indirectly through the denominational machinery.

Another possible choice for the contributor is the *faith mission* (also known as nondenominational or interdenominational). This independent mission may be a well-organized mission with a long history of effective work and with a good reputation of Christian service. Such a group will have a well-established board of directors which sets its policies and in general sees that its work is carried on "decently and in order." There are two basic types of control in these missions. Some are controlled by the missionaries who are members of the mission and elect the directors from among their own number. Others are controlled by a board of directors made up of church leaders and businessmen with some representation from the missionary ranks. The independent mission may range in size from around 2,000 missionaries to ten or less.

Still another type of mission can best be described as a *family mission.* Typically, one man is the founder, director, and/or president, while his wife is secretary and/or treasurer, and some close friend is the other officer. There may also be one or two nominal board members. Not infrequently this type of mission puts out the most glowing reports and emotional appeals.

It is especially important here to secure enough financial data to evaluate the cost of solicitation and of overhead in the administration of the group. It has been known for fund raisers for such groups to serve on commission, taking as much as fifty percent of the money collected. From the remaining fifty percent the headquarters still has to get a percentage for administration.

There are also Roman Catholic missions with general names which are not readily distinguishable from evangelical missions, and whose literature fails to identify their creed. They sometimes advertise that their missionaries donate their time without salary. There is no clue that they do this because they are members of religious orders who have taken the vow of poverty.

The contributor confronted with this array of options needs some guidelines to help him decide. This information is shared here not to discourage giving but to challenge sincere donors to careful stewardship. There are great needs and great opportunities that are being met with efficiency and effectiveness. With reasonable care, the contributor can choose organizations which will wisely use the Lord's money and will provide a real satisfaction for the giver.

The kind of mission that should be supported has certain characteristics which can usually be determined by reasonable care and curiosity by the donor. It is important to find an organization that has a good reputation. When there are constant questions and rumors circulating, it is especially important to be cautious. A solid mission should have a board of directors which is not made up of family members and which has some real control over the organization's affairs. The mission's finance and work reports should be accurate and subject to scrutiny without embarrassment.

There are a number of practical steps a donor may take to evaluate an organization and determine whether he wants to contribute to its program.

1.  Check with a trusted pastor or Christian leader for his evaluation of the organization.
2.  Check to see whether the mission is a member of an association of missions such as the Evangelical Foreign Missions Association, the Interdenominational Foreign Mis-

sion Association, or the Fellowship of Missions.[2] These "umbrella" agencies require their members to meet certain standards and to submit financial reports.

3. Ask for a statement of faith to which the organization adheres.

4. Ask the mission organization for a financial statement for the previous year which will give a breakdown of income and expenses. Seek to determine from the statement how much of the money is fulfilling the objectives of the organization. If the mission seems insulted about the request, that in itself may answer your question.

5. Ask for a list of the members of the board of directors, their church affiliation, and the method by which they are chosen.

6. Beware of extravagant, unrealistic claims about results. Unreasonably low figures for supporting "native" workers can be a clue.

There are many spiritually mature organizations which are operated by Spirit-filled leaders for the glory of God. With reasonable care the supporter can enter into a very rewarding team effort providing crucial support to dynamic and ongoing ministries. This word of caution about a very tiny questionable element should not distract you from the great work that is being faithfully done by the majority of missions and missionaries.

## SCRIPTURE LESSON

"And from there they sailed to Antioch, from which they had been commended to the grace of God for the work that they had accomplished. And when they had arrived and gathered the church together, they *began* to report all things that God had done with them and how He had opened a door of faith to the Gentiles. And they spent a long time with the disciples" (Ac 14:26-28).

"And not only this, but he has also been appointed by the

churches to travel with us in this gracious work, which is being administered by us for the glory of the LORD Himself, and to *show* our readiness, taking precaution that no one should discredit us in our administration of this generous gift; for we have regard for what is honorable, not only in the sight of the LORD, but also in the sight of men" (2 Co 8:19-21).

## DISCUSSION QUESTIONS

1. List the categories of missions mentioned in the chapter.
2. Under each category list the names of the missions you can recall.
3. Name the publications which they provide to donors and prospective donors. Do they ever publish financial reports? Have you ever studied one?
4. As a class project, let each member bring appeal letters, mission papers, financial reports and other material about missions. Examine and discuss them in class.
5. From the finance report can you determine how much goes into overhead? How much for institutional work, direct evangelism, and other types of work?
6. Suppose a young person from your church is called to serve with a mission which you are not accustomed to supporting. Will the church help him financially? How will you determine whether the mission is worthy of support? If the church is to help him, will it be by church action or through the gifts of individuals?

# 10

## HOW SHOULD WE PAY OUR MISSIONARIES?

"DILIGENTLY HELP Zenas the lawyer and Apollos on their way so that nothing is lacking for them. And let our people also learn to engage in good deeds to meet pressing needs, that they may not be unfruitful" (Titus 3:13-14).

This word to Titus by the apostle Paul concerning the missionary trip of this evangelistic team seems to embody the concept of missionary support that generally prevails today. Meeting the missionary's needs is an appropriate goal for Christians and should still be our aim.

The question which arises is how to best accomplish that purpose in today's world. While the need, as well as the desire, to help are constant, the methods for their accomplishment need revision according to prevailing circumstances.

In Luke 10, Jesus sent out witnessing teams and instructed them to take no provisions; yet in Luke 22, speaking of their work following His death, Jesus instructed them to go well provisioned. This would seem to imply that Jesus viewed methods of support to be adaptable according to the situation. Paul was flexible also. At times he worked at making tents commercially; at other times he received support from remote churches.

Historically, many methods of support have characterized the modern missionary movement. Nondenominational missions have generally depended on *designated* or *personalized* giving. Under this system, the missionary makes contacts through relatives, friends, or churches and secures the backing of people who will agree to provide a certain amount toward his support during the four or five years he will spend overseas in missionary service. When enough people have made such a commitment, he is sent out.

The supporters send their contributions to the mission, and these are applied toward his living allowance and other expenses. This money is handled in a number of ways by the organization under which he serves. It is quite common for the mission to receive a specified amount or percentage for administrative costs to cover the home office. Transportation to and from the field must be met. In some missions the money is pooled, and each missionary receives a share. In other cases the mission sets a ceiling. If more comes in than is allowed by the ceiling, it is held back to be applied at a time when the money might not come in; or at the missionary's request it might be transferred to work funds to be used for projects on the field.

Another pattern of giving involves commitments by congregations. A congregation will determine that it will support a missionary by giving a specified amount on a regular basis. Individuals in the church contribute to the fund to meet this commitment.

Direct mail appeals may seek money to be administered by the organization, or money for the support of a specified missionary or project.

Within all of these systems there are certain approaches and patterns which have traditional backgrounds and are very binding in many cases. Some groups consider it very unspiritual to mention specific needs or in any way vocalize a request for support or funds. They speak of projects and needs in a general way, but refuse to request help. Others feel that it is proper Christian stewardship to present their need in a forthright manner, suggesting that their friends and supporters share in their ministry for the Lord.

In a recent article in *Eternity*, Eric Fife approaches this problem gingerly. He begins by giving the view of Hudson Taylor, founder of the China Inland Mission:

> Taylor was convinced that, without any guaranteed support, God would meet his mission's financial needs. The missionaries would not be guaranteed a salary, but the money that the Lord sent in would be shared among the missionaries. He insisted that offerings should never be taken at his meetings. Furthermore, he specified that all salaries would be equal. The youngest recruit would receive as much as the director or as a doctor.[1]

Fife notes that in the United States, "mission boards began requiring new recruits to raise their own support from personal contacts and sympathetic churches. This at least served the purpose of guaranteeing a minimal salary level; coming, as I did, from England where allowances are often pittances, this seemed like a wonderful improvement."[2]

Fife also mentions one of the drawbacks of this system which is, "its failure to supply adequate retirement provisions. After all, who is interested in supporting retired missionaries?"[3]

> Frankly, I do not know what the solution will be. A decade ago it would have seemed unspiritual to question the faith mission approach to finances. But we must take seriously Paul's injunction to Timothy: "But if anyone does not make provision for his own relatives, and especially for the members of his own household, he has denied the faith and is worse than an unbeliever." We need to give this matter intensive study and to be open to major changes if the problems of faith mission financing are to be corrected.[4]

Within a denominational organizational pattern, missions money generally comes from member churches. It may come as a part of the local church budget, as a result of personal pledges at an annual missionary convention, or through personalized or designated giving through the congregations to the national headquarters.

By whatever method, missionary money does come in. The next question is how to arrange for its distribution into the work to be accomplished.

In the early days of modern missions, person-to-person giving was very common. People would simply hand money to the missionary or mail it to him after he departed. This involved no coordination or direction.

As more missionaries went out, missionary societies came into being to serve the missionary efforts. A system of *pooled* support developed as a group of missionaries and their supporters would work together. The contributors would put their gifts into the common fund, and each participating missionary would receive his share. Some variations of this plan are still in operation.

It is more common today for the mission organization to receive the contributions as *designated* amounts for the work of a certain missionary. The mission sets the amounts that will be disbursed as *living allowance* or *salary*. Funds are set aside for the operation of the mission itself as well as for the work projects overseas.

Missions convey this information to their contributors in various ways. The samples provided show the breakdown of the missionary dollar as presented to the public by two groups. The history and tradition of the mission affects the way items are labeled. As you study the meaning of various items in the two samples, you will realize that the use of the dollar is quite similar even though presented in a different way.

### Breakdown of the Missions Dollar

| Sample 1 | Sample 2 |
|---|---|
| Missionary allowance (salary) ..........33¢ | Missionary allowance (salary) ..........33¢ |
| Retirement ..........08 | Medical .............02 |
| Medical insurance ....04 | Missionary travel .....04 |
| Travel on field .......03 | Field expense ........26 |
| Field and housing expense ..........28 | Administration .......10 |
| Furlough expense ....10 | Promotion ..........05 |
| Administration and promotion .........14 | Ministry to US churches ..........08 |
|  | Miscellaneous ........01 |

Regardless of how the money is raised, the method of payment to the missionary most commonly used is a system of *allowances*. It is also a general practice to allow the missionary to solicit funds for an *outfit* before leaving for his place of service. This is to buy equipment which is difficult to secure at his place of assignment. In some cases, people give actual items of equipment or clothing to make up the outfit. There is also the *transportation account* which must be in reserve to cover the round-trip fare to the place of service. Once he is fully supported, the missionary goes out. He receives a series of allowances to meet the needs of the family. He generally receives *living* allowances for basic food requirements and *children's* allowances for food for the children. There may also be *servant* allowances, *fuel* allowances, *laundry* allowances, *yard* allowances and other items of a similar nature. It is a complex system that has developed around the concept of providing expenses for the missionary but not giving him a salary. The complexity of the situation is increased by the fact that the economy is different in each nation and the cost of living varies widely.

Some missions have concluded that this system has become too complex and are attempting to simplify the whole matter. A few pioneering leaders have introduced a system which is sometimes called a "balance sheet" approach to compensation. To begin with, a basic salary figure is chosen. One mission adopted as its base salary the beginning salary of a teacher in a nearby public high school. Another did an elaborate survey of pastors' salaries. After introducing numerous other factors, they arrived at a base salary. From this amount the mission subtracts those things which are normally paid for by the individual, but in the case of the missionary will be supplied by the mission, such as: housing, car (if one is supplied), and the equivalent of income tax, since the missionary does not pay tax as a resident overseas. (If he must pay tax there on the field, the mission pays it for him.) To this is added a cost-of-living adjustment, if it is needed because of the economy where he is.

This salary replaces the living allowance, the children's allowances, and other allowances. To compensate to some extent for the loss of the children's allowances, experience-related yearly increases (up to twelve years) are given. The missionary now determines the rate of additions to the family within the framework of this salary. The salary and the annual increases are the same regardless of the number of children.

An example of compensation for a new missionary family in one mission that is changing to a balance sheet or total compensation approach is shown.

### Compensation for New Missionary Family
#### (1973)

| | | |
|---|---:|---:|
| Total compensation | | 9,488 |
| Less noncash items: | | |
| housing | 2100 | |
| automobile | 800 | |
| social security | 688 | |
| medical benefits | 500 | |
| equipment | 400 | |
| personal gifts | 200 | −4,688 |
| Basic allowance or salary | | 4,800 |

The total compensation figure will vary, depending on the decision of the board. The noncash items taken away will vary depending on items which are provided for the missionary by his mission. The mission in the example shown gives an annual increase of $100 to the family for the first ten years. Some spread the *service increment* increases over a twenty-year period.

In the case of one mission switching over to this system (in 1972), the actual salary of a missionary family will range from $400 to $600 monthly, depending on variables of vehicle ownership and years of experience.

In addition to the salary, *service support* funds must be raised. The mission administers the expenses which are not salary, such as: group life insurance, a health plan, a modest retirement plan, social security, and workmen's compensation (required by law in some states).

The salary plus the service support equals the support income needed by the missionary family. In the case mentioned above this averages out at about $800 per month per family. On the average, about 60 percent of this support income is sent to the missionary family as salary. The remainder goes for service support as outlined above, plus furlough transportation and administrative services provided by the mission. Supporters will be given a *support income* figure as the amount that must be secured to maintain that missionary on active duty.

Such an approach used in conjunction with cost-of-living tables—available through the Evangelical Foreign Missions Association and the Interdenominational Foreign Mission Association from an industrial service—enables the mission to equalize the purchasing power of missionaries in various parts of the world. This equalization process is a complex matter which has been inadequately dealt with in the past, but today tools are available which help to resolve it.

The economic upheaval around the world that led to the price freeze in the United States in 1971 and to the devaluation of the dollar dramatized the unresponsiveness of the traditional systems of missionary support.

### Rise in Cost of Living, Spring, 1971, to Spring, 1973

| | | | |
|---|---|---|---|
| Japan | 33% | Peru | 18% |
| Germany | 30% | Korea | 18% |
| Zaire (Congo) | 30% | Brazil | 17% |
| Ivory Coast | 25% | India | 16% |

The percentages given in the accompanying list depict the approximate rise in the cost of living for an American receiving his allowance in dollars. The change is a combination of devaluation and revaluation of currencies, plus a degree of inflation in the country involved.

For missions that have not changed, the prevailing system is for missionaries in each country to send in reports at set intervals on the cost of food where they live. Their report is averaged out with those of others serving with the same mission, and an allowance is established by the mission board in the United States. Frequently this is done for each country independently, with no provision for keeping equity among the various countries. In some other missions, all missionaries are paid the same dollar amount regardless of the economic conditions of the country of their adoption.

More missions are wrestling with the problem and endeavoring to find some system which will provide for more responsiveness to the fluctuating economy and currency in the country where the missionary serves.

Within the existing systems of missionary support there is the problem of securing an *outfit*. Frequently women's missionary groups buy outfit items of clothing, household items, appliances, toys, etc., for the outgoing missionary. This has considerable appeal to the groups doing it, but it does become problematical at times. Getting proper fits, adequate quality, and appropriate materials and styles for the climate overseas can be difficult. With world commerce being what it is today, it is sometimes more practical to take money and secure goods overseas. It is conceivable that, in rounding up an outfit, a missionary will be given a shirt which was made in Hong Kong to take with him to Asia, a bit of unnecessary shipping to say the least.

Under the more progressive *salary* systems, the outfit concept is also done away with or minimized. The missionary plans his purchases as any other family. He decides what to buy in the United States and what he may buy more effectively overseas.

How does all of this relate to the matter of Internal Revenue Service regulations about deductions for charitable contributions? Generally speaking, in any system in which the mission clearly sets limits on the amount of allowance or salary which is to be passed on to the missionary, the contribution to the mission for him is for the organization and its work. The salary of the missionary is a part of that project of the mission in which he serves. The missionary is carrying out the charitable and religious purposes of the mission and is being paid for it. Within this context, designated giving is generally acceptable to the Internal Revenue.

Some contributors, however, make it difficult for mission organizations when they insist on getting tax deductible receipts for personal gifts such as above-allowance gifts for personal use or for family use. The mission should not be expected to give receipts for gifts to missionary children, gifts for birthdays or Christmas, gifts for vacations, gifts for children's education. These items are not for the charitable and religious functions of the mission. Such items are gifts to and for the use of individuals and are not permitted as deductible contributions by IRS.

This study should not conclude without mention of an increasingly delicate problem in the area of support. As missions move toward more adequate systems of missionary support from the United States perspective, the difference in economic status between the missionary and pastors in the countries where they serve becomes greater. This places a burden on him in terms of identification with the people to whom he ministers. Increased sensitivity to this problem is necessary and solutions must be sought.

## Scripture Lesson

"And He was saying to them, 'The harvest is plentiful, but the laborers are few; therefore beseech the LORD of the harvest to send out laborers into His harvest. Go your ways; behold, I send you out as lambs in the midst of wolves. Carry no purse, no bag, no shoes; and greet no one on the way'" (Lk 10:2-4).

"And He said to them, 'When I sent you out without purse and bag and sandals, you did not lack anything, did you?' And they said, 'No, nothing.' And He said to them, 'But now, let him who has a purse take it along, likewise also a bag, and let him who has no sword sell his robe and buy one'" (Lk 22:35-36).

## Discussion Questions

1. Describe and discuss the methods generally used by *nondenominational* and *interdenominational* missions to finance their personnel, their work projects and institutions.
2. Describe the methods generally used by denominational missions to finance their missionary work.
3. Discuss the system of allowance used to provide the missionary's living expenses. Note the advantages and disadvantages. Make suggestions for improving the system.
4. Do a role-playing project. Constitute yourselves into the field conference of country A. You are the total missionary staff of a given mission in that country. The United States headquarters has told you to figure out what the basic living allowance should be for your field. Decide how you will proceed to arrive at a single figure which every family should get.

5. How would your women's missionary group feel about not having the opportunity to be involved in providing an outfit for missionaries going to the field?

# 11

## THE LOCAL CHURCH AND MISSIONS

SUPPORT AND PERSONNEL for the world outreach of North American Protestantism springs primarily from local congregations of believers. In some cases the support money and personnel are channeled almost entirely through denominational structures. In the case of interdenominational missions the process of securing money and recruits is more nebulous. A number of factors influence the procedure: personal contacts, direct mail appeals, interdenominational missionary prayer groups, and numerous other factors. The dominant factor, however, in the long run is the interest and backing of pastors.

Where a pastor is interested in missions or a particular mission, he can strongly influence the involvement and activities of the congregation in relation to missions. How pastors and missionary societies relate to each other becomes a matter of vital importance in this context. Some tensions have begun to surface which could disrupt the cordial relationship which is needed.

Some pastors, especially those surrounded by business and professional men trained in management techniques, are beginning to ask questions about the structures of missions:

How are they organized? Who is on the controlling board? Does the mission have clear objectives? Are they evaluating their progress?

A report from Great Britain speaks of this matter.

> Another of Philip Crowe's suggestions is that "missionary societies would benefit greatly if their committees were properly elected by supporters," instead of, as in many cases, appointing themselves. There are practical difficulties, but in the climate of thought of Britain in the 70's, when people expect to have some responsibility for the running of organizations they are called upon to support, some changes will have to come. "Even if elections do not prove practical, something must be done to lower the average age of council members. This may mean changing the time of the meetings, or the retirement age, and will certainly involve a determined search for new blood."[1]

Since a mission is frequently supported by hundreds of churches scattered geographically across the country, how can each church and pastor become involved in the decision-making process? In most missions some pastors are on the controlling board, but since they are unrelated to other supporting churches, they cannot really represent them. Pastors and missions leaders need to give serious thought to this problem and come up with some new approaches.

In another area, pastors have expressed concern about what they feel is competitive pressure for their missionary dollar and for their young people. A church which is known to be heavily committed to missions is bombarded with frequent requests to allow missionaries to speak and make appeals for support. The pastor may well feel that his people are already committed to all they can support. He may turn down the request, or he may allow the missionary to speak, with an honorarium for the service but no opportunity to present projects or personal support needs.

In such a situation the missionary who is responsible to

secure his full support and transportation for the next five years wonders out loud how people will be able to respond to his needs under these circumstances.

Missions leaders and pastors must continue to work on improving communications in these areas so that solutions can be found.

Discussing still another area of tension, pastors have expressed concern about how their people can get a full and adequate view of missions. Obviously, the individual missionary is burdened about, and presents, the work in his restricted geographical area and his organizational contact. He, unfortunately, may not have a broad knowledge of world missions or even activities of other groups in his own country. Furthermore, his reporting is influenced by what he thinks will get prayer support and financial backing for his work.

He is also influenced by what he thinks people want to hear. It is common (perhaps with some reason) for the missionary to feel that people want to hear extraordinary and thrilling stories. He thinks people want to hear of things that are exotic and primitive. If he lives in a modern metropolis and fights rush hour traffic to get to his literature office or his downtown radio station, what can he tell? This is the missionary's dilemma when he faces the church.

From their side, the people and pastor are saying, "Do the missionaries carry on their work in the same way they did in the nineteenth century? When Japan is supplying the world with radios and television sets, what modern techniques do the missionaries use to reach Japan? Do churches overseas have the problems of metropolitan churches of North America? Do new Christians there have the same kinds of struggles that North American believers wrestle with?"

Is it possible for the missionary to give a well-rounded view of the church and Christians overseas? To resolve growing concern in this area, ways must be sought to provide the missionary with a more realistic view of the pastor's problems and to provide the pastor with a more adequate understanding of missions in today's world.

One step toward a solution may be to have the individual missionary more personally involved with a local home church. This involvement could begin with the training of the new candidate. Arrangements could be made to have a missionary candidate serve several months, or a couple of years, in active ministry in a supporting church just before leaving for his assignment overseas. The sending mission should work out the program with the pastor to provide experiences which will be meaningful on the field. The pastor and congregation become actively involved in the evaluation of this candidate for service. The people will be able to provide prayer support of a very personal sort after having known the missionary in this way.

With the rapid pace of change in the North American culture today, the missionary returning from four or five years of service abroad needs some orientation for "re-entry." Here again, the pastor of a supporting church is the ideal person to provide such help. A few weeks of work with the pastor upon return could reacquaint the missionary with the people, reveal their needs and problems, and prepare him for fruitful homeland contacts.

Another way to cement relationships between the pastor and missionary is for the pastor to visit the overseas work of the mission. Churches that have very large missionary commitments find it profitable to send the pastor to see personally what is happening overseas. A few days of involvement in the work of the missionary can do more to make him feel the pulse of the ministry than any number of talks and pictures. He, in turn, will communicate to the congregation that which has become an important experience for him. While visiting the overseas work, he may have crucial opportunities to provide pastoral care for the missionary, his family, and perhaps fellow missionaries.

Some pastors have raised the question of local churches and pastors here making contact with local congregations in overseas countries. Such a concept has been likened to a secular program of sister cities in which visits are arranged between leaders of cities of similar size in the United States and another country. They become concerned and involved in each other's problems. They share insights and may arrange aid programs.

Would it be feasible, pastors ask, to make such an arrangement with a Third World church? Some visits might be made, correspondence carried on, and other involvement encouraged. Pastors seem enthusiastic about the idea. Missions tend to be reluctant, as questions come to mind. Would not such a program tend to emphasize and establish inter-church aid to the detriment of evangelism? Would there not be a danger of aiding in constructing great buildings, and other United States-style projects instead of aiding thrusts into unreached populations? Would aid reaching some families and not others create unrest among the church family?

After being involved in the sessions and workshops at a study conference on "Missions in Creative Tension," pastor Lud Golz of Wheaton, Illinois jotted down his meditations on the matter of relationships.

> As a result of my involvement in GL '71 I plan to take specific action on the following: (1) Be more specific in my correspondence with our missionaries in asking them what we as a church want to know (maybe enclosing a questionnaire which would be easy for them to answer), (2) The next time I get a reference blank from a mission regarding a candidate from my church, I will bring it up to the congregation so they can express themselves and send a report of their response to the mission, (3) Develop a section in our church library with pertinent information to help missionaries adjust to the home scene while on furlough, and counsel with them early in their furlough to help in this area, (4) Encourage my church to share me with the missionaries we

support and the national church abroad, (5) Be available to mission leaders to work on church-mission relationship.[2]

For the missions, pastors have provided some suggestions on how to grapple with some of the problems. To reduce the competition for the church's money and personnel, pastors have suggested the merger of some missions. In their view it would create more efficient operations with less overhead. Studies need to be made to determine whether this is indeed true.

Here is the candid observation of the missions commission of the Evangelical Alliance (Great Britain) in a recent report:

> Missionary societies should thoroughly overhaul their control structures at home and overseas. There needs to be a marked reduction in the average age of many mission councils and committees. It is a little short of ludicrous that groups of aged or middle-aged men and women should sit in London (or New York or wherever) and attempt to control the witness of the Gospel to, say, the people of Singapore, half of whom are under 21. The undoubted wisdom and experience of the older generation needs the infusion of contemporary attitudes and enthusiasms which can only come from members of the younger generation.[3]

Another section of the same report observed that,

> missionary societies will still have a vital part to play in the foreseeable future. But some radical changes will also be needed. We must recognize the difficulties in the present system and seek ways of eliminating them or reducing their effect. . . . As we have seen, much closer cooperation, if not complete amalgamation, will be almost essential. We suggest that the pattern we should aim at is to have fewer societies in two groups:
>
> a. Missions that concentrate on geographical areas. It could be the best plan to have just one evangelical missionary society for, say, the Indian subcontinent, East Asia, Latin America, Sub-Saharan Africa, the Middle East and North

Africa, and Europe; though some of these areas might be
divided.
b. Missions that concentrate on specialist functions, acting
as service agencies in fields such as radio and television,
literature, leprosy work, youth work, and so on.[4]

Some missions are taking steps to develop closer ties with
supporting churches. Some have formed or strengthened a
church-ministries department in the mission. These take positive action to aid churches in their missionary emphasis by
providing planning helps, materials, and personnel. Pastors
become more involved with mission executives in conferences
and strategy meetings, which increases their mutual understanding.

In many churches, missionary committees actively conduct
missionary education throughout the Christian Education
structure. The committee seeks to involve an ever-increasing
number of people in serious prayer for missions. Its program
can be geared to challenging young people to missionary
service, and people of all ages to financial backing. A very
active missionary committee may be involved in arranging
such things as: conducting a conference or convention; year-
round teaching through the Sunday school and other Christian education activities; providing audio visuals; arranging
small missionary groups for study and prayer, dramatizations,
special cantatas, and bulletin boards.

An extensive manual became available in 1973 to help local
churches organize their missions program.[5] It outlines procedures and lists many sources for additional material. Local
churches can also obtain a wide variety of missions information by subscribing to the services of Evangelical Missions
Information Service.[6]

## Scripture Lesson

"And from there they sailed to Antioch, from which they
had been commended to the grace of God for the work that
they had accomplished. And when they had arrived and

gathered the church together, they began to report all things that God had done with them and how He had opened a door of faith to the Gentiles. And they spent a long time with the disciples" (Ac 14:26-28).

"And when they arrived at Jerusalem, they were received by the church and the apostles and the elders, and they reported all that God had done with them. But certain ones of the sect of the Pharisees who had believed, stood up, saying, 'It is necessary to circumcise them, and to direct them to observe the Law of Moses.' And the apostles and the elders came together to look into this matter" (Ac 15:4-6).

"And Judas and Silas, also being prophets themselves, encouraged and strengthened the brethren with a lengthy message. And after they had spent time *there*, they were sent away from the brethren in peace to those who had sent them out. But Paul and Barnabas stayed in Antioch, teaching and preaching, with many others also, the word of the LORD" (Ac 15:32-35).

## DISCUSSION QUESTIONS

1. Is the missionary interest in your church strongly influenced by the pastor?

2. Do you have a missions committee? Is most of the church's missionary giving channeled through the committee?

3. As a group project, you may want to secure the cooperation of the missions committee to do a survey (anonymous) to find out how much money is given directly to missionary agencies without coming through the church.

4. Describe the structure of the missions that you or your church support.

5. List advantages and disadvantages of merging some of the smaller missions.

6. What do you think of the recommendation that pastors be sent to visit a mission field? One pastor said it would be a good investment of missionary funds. Do you agree?

7.  Discuss the concept of having a sister church on a mission field. List potential blessings and potential hazards.

8.  Some churches have found that encouraging one of their young people to be involved in short-term missionary service stimulates missionary interest. Do you know anyone who has gone in this capacity?

# 12

## THIRD WORLD MISSIONS

CHRISTIANS in North America are gradually becoming aware of the development of missionary societies in countries which are traditional mission fields. As this awareness dawns, people begin to raise questions about this activity. Some questions are reminiscent of the detractors of missions in North America, Europe, and other sending countries. Why should the new churches on the "field" send missionaries to other countries when their own country has not been evangelized?

It seems fair to answer in the same way that critics in the traditional sending countries have been answered. The Word to all Christians everywhere at all times during the church age is the same: "But you shall receive power when the Holy Spirit has come upon you; and you shall be My witnesses both in Jerusalem, and in all Judea and Samaria, and even to the remotest part of the earth" (Ac 1:8).

Since this activity is to be the work of the Holy Spirit in the Church, it is not incongruous to suppose that a church at any stage of development will be carrying on its witness locally, at nearby places and out beyond international boundaries. There is nothing to say that evangelization of the local areas must be completed before missionary efforts can be undertaken. On the contrary, the Christians in the book of Acts sent out missionary teams while the churches in Jerusalem, Judea, and Samaria were still in their infancy.

Strangely enough, in spite of having been forced to over-come the objections of the detractors of missions themselves, many missionaries have instilled in the churches born of their labors those very objections. In recent years, however, some missions have begun to stimulate deliberately the newer churches to send their representatives to other countries. Churches which have undertaken such projects, even on a small scale, have found that it has stimulated evangelistic zeal in the sending churches and at the same time it stirs interest in supporting missions.

Where the vision has developed, it becomes necessary to determine a procedure to carry out this activity. Some have adopted the method which has been quite common in North America. A denomination (or association of churches) in a given country will set up a mission board responsible to the church leadership. This board will set standards, recruit candidates, raise funds, and find places of service. Proponents of this system feel that it is a suitable way for churches to become fully involved. The churches are supporting *their* missionaries and from this obedience they harvest the spiritual rewards. There is also the human satisfaction of doing a significant work on their own.

Christian and Missionary Alliance churches have made significant beginnings in such programs around the world. The Alliance churches of the Philippines now have missionaries serving in Indonesia; those of Japan in Brazil. Missionaries have gone from Vietnam to Laos and from Argentina to Uruguay. Hong Kong churches have twenty missionaries serving in Cambodia, Indonesia, Vietnam, Peru, Canada, and England. These five Christian and Missionary Alliance agencies together send sixty missionaries. They have formed a fellowship and publish a paper called *The Asian Missionary Trumpet*.

Describing their feeling at the beginning of a missions program, the president of the Christian and Missionary Alliance churches of the Philippines reported:

> Admittedly, insofar as the young church of the Philippines is concerned, the foreign missions venture was the first—the first candidates, the first assignment, the first field, the first experience with regard to legal papers and all ramifications that come along with the visa and passport problems. This was also the first taste and challenge for the sending church.[1]

On fund raising the Philippine president reported:

> When the first missionary couple went to Indonesia, the women had drums full of missionary supplies. In addition, they gave their pledges regularly. Generally, in the Philippines, mothers or wives hold the pocketbook of the family. See what it means to have Christian women mission conscious?[2]

Mr. F. L. Kamasi, a leader of the Christian and Missionary Alliance in Indonesia, describes the relationship between the receiving church in Indonesia and the sending church in the Philippines: "At the invitation of the Indonesian church, the Philippine national church began to make arrangements for a Filipino couple to come to Indonesia."[3]

Mr. Kamasi stated, "the relationship of the missionary to the sending body, the Philippine national church, is that he is responsible to it for support, direction, and regulations it sets up for its missionaries."[4]

Guidelines on the relationship state that,

> missionaries will work under the direction of the national (Indonesian) church. The location of these missionaries will be decided by the Indonesian national church executive committee who will appoint them to one of the seven KINGMI (C&MA of Indonesia) regions and then the region will be responsible to determine the specific area of service within that area. The cost of living and the cost of transportation is the direct responsibility of the sending church.[5]

This situation adds a new wrinkle to the question of church-mission relationships. In Indonesia there are autonomous churches which have a relationship to North American missionaries who serve there and to Philippine missionaries who also serve there.

The Africa Mission Society of the Evangelical Churches of West Africa (ECWA) has chosen a similar pattern. This is the mission society of the 1,200 churches raised up in Nigeria as the result of the work of the Sudan Interior Mission. The Africa Mission Society is a department of the ECWA church organization. An elected Nigerian secretary processes the missionary applications and carries on administrative work. In the traditional use of the terms, this society handles both home and foreign missions. However, most of the "home" missionaries go to another tribe within Nigeria where they face the problems of language and culture, even though they remain within the political boundaries of Nigeria. In October, 1971, the ECWA Africa Mission Society had in its service 194 missionaries supported by the constituent churches in Nigeria and directed by Nigerian leaders.[6]

The Overseas Missionary Fellowship (formerly the China Inland Mission) has taken a different approach to stimulate missionary activity among the churches it serves overseas. The development of a distinctive approach is described by Arthur Glasser:

> The real tragedy is that the Christian church has been so delinquent in manifesting its essential oneness—a oneness transcending racial, color, cultural, and national barriers. This awareness brought our conference to its crisis. Crucial questions were asked. Why should the Overseas Missionary Fellowship not cut loose from its western moorings, reject its Caucasian stance before a racially divided world, and open its doors to all who are called of God to embrace the missionary calling? Why should it not offer itself to the churches of Asia, in the same way that it has offered itself to the churches of the West as a vehicle through which they might

discharge their missionary responsibility? Why not pray for
the early entrance of qualified Asians to all administrative
levels of OMF's structures so that this fellowship might
speedily demonstrate itself as neither western nor eastern,
but rather a demonstration of the oneness that there is in
Jesus Christ? For several days we grappled with these questions, then made the decision, for the glory of God and in
response to His evident leading. A "new" OMF was begotten
from its aged parent.[7]

Glasser also reported that Asians "feel this will give Asian
churches a new sense of stewardship, and release in them a
dynamism for sacrificial service not hitherto demonstrated."
Since starting that policy, the Overseas Missionary Fellowship has received such missionaries into its ranks. There are
Filipino missionaries serving in Indonesia and Japan; Chinese
from Hong Kong serving in Laos and Indonesia; a Malaysian
and an Indian serving in Thailand.

A home council of the Overseas Missionary Fellowship is
formed in each sending country to serve in channeling its
nationals into the overall work of the society. It provides a
way for finances to be forwarded to the missionary and seeks
prayer backing for him.

In another innovation, the Latin America Mission has
adopted a new form of organization. It places major responsibility for the continuation and development of its highly
diversified ministries in the hands of Latin American Christian
leaders at the point of action. The new structure provides
for an international organization to be known as the Comuni-
dad Latino Americano de Ministerios Evangelicos (Community of Latin American Evangelical Ministries). It takes the
form of a federation of autonomous entities, in which Latin
American leadership is prominent. The Latin America Mission, United States, is one among the various "communities."

Missions being formed in the countries which have historically been the object of missionary work are referred to as
Third World missions. *Third World* is not a specifically de-

fined term, but in general usage it seems to refer mainly to
Africa, Asia, and Latin America. It is generally believed to
have developed to describe those who did not want to be
aligned with the West or with the Communist powers, so they
used the term *Third World*.

Efforts to gather information about the activities of Third
World missions reveal the need for developing terminology
that will make it possible to collect data compatible with facts
which have been gathered in the older sending countries. So
far, the United States distinction between home and foreign
missions has not worked out too well in the international
arena.

A study of Third World missions, described by the authors
as "a very preliminary effort," has turned up the most complete information that has been collected on the subject.

In gathering data for the book *Missions from the Third
World*, the following definition was used in the questionnaire:
"By 'missionary' we mean: an individual sent from one country or location to serve in another, with the ultimate purpose
of seeing the Body of Christ established and growing in that
area."[8]

Given the definition, it is not surprising that the survey
turned up some groups which in the United States have tra-
ditionally been called home missions. For example, a person
going from New York to Arizona to work among Indians
would meet that definition.

*Missions from the Third World* reports on 203 missions
based in forty-six Third World countries having a combined
total of 2,971 missionaries. Recognizing the incompleteness
of the survey on which the book is based, the authors estimate
the missionaries to number 3,404.[9]

Japan reported thirty-two agencies, some of which have
formed themselves into the Japan Overseas Missions Association (JOMA). Brazil reported twenty-six agencies with 495
missionaries. Many work among minorities within Brazil, but

a good number have gone to other Latin American countries and to Portugal.

In Korea, a total of seven missions have been organized to send Koreans to other parts of the world. They have also formed the Korea Foreign Missions Association to foster co-operation among the groups.

In view of the rapidly developing mission agencies in their part of the world, Asian church and mission leaders called an "All Asia Mission Consultation," held in August, 1973, in Seoul, Korea. It was called and conducted by Asians; but, in a spirit of fellowship, a few mission leaders from other parts of the world were invited as observers. Participants from Asia numbered about thirty-six, representing about twelve countries.

The thrust of the conference was the responsibility of the Asian churches to take seriously the mission mandate—by supporting personnel to go beyond their boundaries to share Christ. They established as their immediate goal the sending of 200 new missionaries during 1974. They appointed a continuing committee to plan future projects, including establishment of a missionary orientation and research center.

The men gathered for the All Asia Mission Consultation made it clear that they do not see themselves as replacing missionaries who come from other parts of the world. They envision a truly international, interracial missionary force that will cooperate in the task of evangelizing the world.

It is an exciting prospect!

## SCRIPTURE LESSON

"Now there were at Antioch, in the church that was *there,* prophets and teachers: Barnabas, and Simeon who was called Niger, and Lucius of Cyrene, and Manaen who had been brought up with Herod the tetrarch, and Saul. And while they were ministering to the LORD and fasting, the Holy Spirit said, 'Set apart for Me Barnabas and Saul for the work to which I have called them.' Then, when they had fasted and prayed and laid their hands on them, they sent them away. So, being sent out by the Holy Spirit, they went down to Seleucia and from there they sailed to Cyprus. And when they reached Salamis, they *began* to proclaim the word of God in the synagogues of the Jews; and they also had John as their helper" (Ac 13:1-5).

"And from there they sailed to Antioch, from which they had been commended to the grace of God for the work that they had accomplished. And when they had arrived and gathered the church together, they *began* to report all things that God had done with them and how He had opened a door of faith to the Gentiles. And they spent a long time with the disciples" (Ac 14:26-28).

"So as to preach the gospel even to the regions beyond you, and not to boast in what has been accomplished in the sphere of another" (2 Co 10:16).

## Discussion Questions

1. Discuss the term *Third World*. How do you think the term originated? Does the class have a consensus about what areas of the world it includes?

2. How do you answer people who say that with all the needs in the United States missionaries should not be sent to other countries? Do you think your reasons would prove convincing in Japan, where no more than 2 percent of the population are Christian?

3. Study Mr. Kamasi's statement about the relationship between Philippine missionaries and the Indonesian church. Do you think the policy is a good one? Do you think it should also apply to United States missionaries who go as missionaries to Indonesia?

4. Discuss the definition of *missionary* used in the survey for *Missions from the Third World,* as reported in this chapter. How would you enlarge or refine it?

# 13

## IS THERE STILL A PLACE FOR UNITED STATES MISSIONARIES?

In the rising complexity of the missionary scene today, young people frequently ask whether there is still a need for missionaries overseas. With the maturing national church and the development of training for its leadership, is there a place for new missionaries? If so, what is their role? This question needs to be viewed from several angles.

In certain geographical areas, it is generally conceded that the work of evangelization is far enough along to make this a valid consideration. In that event, there are still opportunities for the well-trained specialist who can provide further training for the local leadership in his specialty. Even where training for preachers and evangelists is well advanced, there are other aspects of training where help is needed.

In most places there should be programs to train the local leaders in the use of the media and even more fundamentally in the development of the media. In Burundi, Africa, for example, there is a strong church. Within the last several years a gospel radio station—Central Africa Broadcasting Company— has been established. The station has not only trained the church leaders of Burundi in the use of radio, but also through a technical school program, it trains Christians in radio technology. Graduates get jobs in secular broadcasting and thus expand the influence of Christians into the mainstream of society. There are many similar opportunities around the world in fields of medicine, education, literature, management, finance, et cetera.

This need for specialization does not by any means rule out the need for missionaries who will give themselves to evangelism and church planting. In considering this need, it is important to look at the overall situation of a country or area.

Let us imagine a country of 50 million population. Suppose it has fifteen Protestant groups established through missionary work. These church bodies range in membership from 5,000 to 20,000, with a combined total membership of 250,000. Through their ministries the churches have a strong influence on four times that number, making about one million which can be called the Christian community. The church with 20,000 members is a rather mature church. It has a seminary, a medical work, several educational establishments; and it is basically autonomous in its church affairs. It is related to a United States-based mission, which seeks to determine whether the time has come to withdraw its missionaries. If not, what kind of relationship should exist?

As missionaries and national church leaders sit down to consider the question, they will want to look at several factors. On the one hand, the church is well able to care for the pastoral needs of its congregation, and also provide church officers who handle its administrative affairs. Is the missionary still needed? From this perspective it would be easy to argue that the time has come for orderly withdrawal of the missionaries.

It is noted, however, by someone involved in the discussion, that all of the Protestant Christians together total no more than 2 percent of the nation's population. The discussion may then lead to a strategy which will call for the continuing work of the mission alongside the national church. The church affairs will be run by the mature national leaders, but missionaries with a burden for winning the lost will be called for. They will cooperate with the church in starting congregations in towns and villages where none exist.

The new churches will become a part of the national church organization as fast as they are formed. The church leaders may also call for media experts to develop an outreach through the press, radio, and TV. These activities will include training programs to develop local leadership. Church growth studies can be made in cooperation with the church to stimulate the desire for outreach and growth.

Most readers have heard dramatic statements to the effect that missionaries are no longer needed, since the Church has been planted in most parts of the world. Those are not necessarily typical of the feelings of all overseas leaders. Many serious and responsible leaders of autonomous national churches want the continued fellowship and assistance of missionaries. It is true, they are calling for some very basic changes both in patterns of service and in the attitude of the missionaries who will serve.

The time has passed when the young, inexperienced missionary can expect to arrive on the scene and become the director of a district and be the "boss" of "native workers" there. Today's missionary must go to his assignment with an attitude which will prepare him to work alongside the leadership of the area and learn from their Christian experience and maturity how to have an effective ministry in that place. He must strive to exercise the gifts of the Spirit so that they will be recognized by his fellow Christians and pressed into service.

Missionaries from the United States are handicapped today because of conditions here. The racism, violence, and immorality of this nation are a troublesome shadow over him, but these factors do not rule him out as a missionary. If the missionary presents himself as the representative of a Christian nation and the spokesman of a better civilization, these problems will be a hindrance to him. If, however, he goes as a representative of Christ holding no brief for his own civilization, but true concern for the things of God, he will be accepted and have a good ministry. Arrogance and self-righteousness are a hindrance to a person of any nationality, perhaps more so in the case of the American because of his nation's prominence in world affairs and past efforts to call it a Christian nation.

The handicap of being an American can be overcome by those who in obedience to Christ give themselves in a selfless ministry to the world in close fellowship with Christians everywhere.

Uncertainty about the need for missionaries does discourage some potential missionaries. But I fear that deeper causes underlie the reluctance of many to enter missionary work. Doubt concerning people's need for Christ takes on two very prominent forms and deters many from service.

One root cause of indifference is the belief that men who are sincere in whatever religion will be accepted of God in the final analysis. On the matter of lagging missionary interest in many churches, *Christianity Today* editorialized:

> At the same time these denominations were deeply infiltrated by those who no longer believed in the uniqueness of Christianity and bowed to Synchretism (as, for example, Colin Williams, dean of Yale Divinity School, who said that what the Buddhist believes in his situation is as good for him as what he himself—Williams—believes in his own situation).[1]

Those who believe that all religions can bring salvation to man have little motivation to go anywhere to share the message of Christ.

Another basic cause of indifference, and even hostility, to missionary outreach is a new form of universalism which is widespread. It teaches that all men are included in the redemption of Christ and will ultimately be saved. Whether they ever hear the Gospel is immaterial. They will be a part of the final redemption anyway, the argument goes. At most, the role of the Church is to inform them of an accomplished fact. It does not in any event change their status.

For the Christian who operates in obedience to Christ's explicit commands, and who acknowledges the lost estate of man, there is still a missionary call and command. In order to provide opportunities for missionary response, it is urgent that missionary societies concentrate on working out proper relationships with existing national churches. Out of good relationships will grow mutual respect and concern. From that concern will come cooperative plans to reach the remaining populations of all nations, including the United States.

It is entirely reasonable that a church in a given country should be both a *receiving* church and a *sending* church. As pointed out in a previous chapter, churches in a number of countries are in that position. It has been rightfully suggested that churches in the Third World could well send missionaries to North America to do missionary work. Certainly there are many effective ministries which could be performed by such an exchange. This still would not rule out the need for Americans to go to other places.

At the Study Conference at Green Lake, Wisconsin, in 1971, Dr. Louis King stated,

> Missionary outreach then is presented as valid, normative, and essential for the New Testament kind of church. On this account, every church should play its rightful part in the evangelization of its own country and participate in worldwide missionary outreach. . . . Indeed, it is a perennial task. We should, therefore, seek to create an atmosphere for church growth, initiative, and self-reliance in the specific tasks of evangelism and mission by both.[2]

In speaking of missionaries who will be welcome to serve with churches in the seventies, Dennis Clark has said, "Western candidates for missionary work in the seventies should surely be men and women who have demonstrated their spiritual gift among their peers. All the New Testament evidence indicates a selection and support of only the best spiritually qualified persons."[3] Clark also said, "Men and women with proven spiritual gifts can serve the Body of Christ in any place at any time."[4]

Michael Griffiths addresses himself to the same question:

> While the theorists and the missiologists argue in their learned journals, the missionary on the ground at grips with the enemy is in no doubt that reinforcements are needed. From almost everywhere comes the call for "more workers."
>
> There is one kind of missionary that everyone wants. That is the person who will identify himself closely with the people to whom he goes, ready to accept the living standards, to follow the customs and use the thought pattern of the country to which he goes, using them to lead men and women to Christ, and helping in planting new congregations in the mushrooming cities and the scattered villages alike. Missionaries who are soul-winners and church-starters are never likely to be redundant.[5]

In addition to direct evangelism and church planting work, missionaries with training and expertise are needed to train others in their specialty. Such training is not conducted with the regularity that seems advisable and prudent. Many highly trained missionaries effectively fulfill their work and would seem to be ideal for training others.

Two factors seem to be at the root of the failure to train. Overwork and money are probably the most widespread hindrances. The technically trained individual who should be a good trainer frequently finds himself badly overworked. He says very sincerely, "I do not have time to train someone else. I can barely make it, without using the time it would take to train someone." To suggest that someday the trainee will relieve the pressure by helping does not sound convincing in the midst of the situation. To overcome this difficulty, some executive planning is essential. The work must be constructed in such a way that his job is to train. Training must be built into the very fabric of the job, so that he regards himself as a trainer who is also working at his specialty.

The second reality which may retard training is the lack of money. Mission financial structure is such that in many instances no money would be available to pay the new technician's salary if the missionary did train him. The church and the mission must do constructive thinking and planning to overcome this problem. A great potential for training exists in writing, book distribution (including bookstore management), broadcasting, administration, medical work, and evangelism/church growth techniques, among others. Short-term resource people and resident missionaries alike may well spend many profitable years in such training programs.

Today's missionary situation has become much more flexible about types of service in which people can participate. Many varieties of short-term service can be provided by young people. Missions, youth groups, and colleges are all involved in providing plans for short-term work. One plan is summer work with a mission. Volunteers for summer service number hundreds every year. The volunteers raise their own support and go to a mission field in a variety of capacities, including evangelistic teams, musical groups, construction teams, secretaries, and a multitude of other activities. In 1971, a survey was taken among missions belonging to the Interdenominational Foreign Mission Association and the Evangelical Foreign Missions Association about the use of summer workers. Fifty-two missions responded to the survey. It was found that fifty-two missions placed 308 short-termers in the summer of 1966. In the summer of 1970 they placed 1,784 summer workers and were projecting at the time of the survey 1,894 for 1971. It is doubtful whether these figures account for half of those who went out.[6]

The survey found that the cost of board and room and transportation amounted to about $820,500 for the summer of 1970. In concluding the report, Mr. Newbrander said, "It appears from the size and scope of the program that it is here to stay—we had better examine our objectives and procedures to make sure we operate at a high degree of effectiveness."[7]

In addition to summer programs, there are many two-year opportunities for those who have skills which can be used. Many missions have specific programs to recruit and use two-year volunteers in many fields of endeavor, such as: teaching, secretarial work, medical work, printing, etc.

There are specialized agencies which help to recruit these special volunteers and channel them to areas of need with agencies which request them.[8]

Sketchy reports indicate that short-term service is a good recruiting tool. A substantial percentage of those who do volunteer work on a field during their college years end up in some type of missionary work after graduation. In addition to recruitment, short-term work usually results in greater missionary interest in the school or church where the young person is involved.

Short-term service is not limited to young people. Many older folks with special skills are donating short periods of time to specific ministries overseas. A surgeon frequently donates a month of time to a mission hospital where he performs valuable procedures, and at the same time he helps to upgrade the training of doctors who serve there. Retired business and professional men can often find a place where valuable service can be rendered.

Christians looking for opportunities for a witness overseas should not overlook the possibility of taking overseas positions with government and industry with the view to witnessing among the community in which they will work. Such service can never be a substitute for specific missionary service, but it can provide an important supporting ministry, and sometimes can reach a segment of the population not being reached by regular missionaries.

Before accepting the lightly spoken cliche "The day of missionaries has passed," consider all facets of the matter and look at the options that are open. It is very likely that God has a place of service for you. Allow Him to send you to fill it.

## Scripture Lesson

"And He gave some *as* apostles, and some *as* prophets, and some *as* evangelists, and some *as* pastors and teachers" (Eph 4:11).

"Through whom we have received grace and apostleship to bring about the obedience of faith among all the Gentiles, for His name's sake" (Ro 1:5).

On work of missionaries see also: Acts 14:22-23; Titus 1:5; Acts 15:41.

## Discussion Questions

1. Seek to determine how a mission can know that it has finished its work in a specified country, and that the time has come to withdraw personnel and finances. Is it when the church reaches a certain membership? If so, how many members? Is it when a certain percentage of the population believes? If so, what percentage? Could the percentage of believers in the United States provide any guidance?

2. What things do you think may influence some young people not to go into missionary work?

3. List reasons why you think missionary service is still needed. Or, list reasons why you think it is not needed.

4. When a national church starts to send out missionaries to other countries, should we stop sending missionaries to their country? List reasons for your answer.

5. List advantages and disadvantages you see in the continuing expansion of short-term missionary programs.

# NOTES

## CHAPTER 1

1. As quoted by J. Brooke Mosley, *Christians in the Technical and Social Revolution of Our Time*, p. 34. Italics added. Used by permission of Forward Movement Publications.
2. Ibid., p. 35. Italics added.
3. Clarence W. Hall, "Which Way the World Council of Churches?" *Reader's Digest*, November, 1971.
4. "The Frankfurt Declaration," *Christianity Today*, June 19, 1970, pp. 843-46. Quoted from Christianity Today by permission.
5. Donald McGavran, "Will Uppsala Betray the Two Billion," *Church Growth Bulletin* 4, no. 5:295.
6. Ibid., p. 296.
7. "The Frankfurt Declaration," *Christianity Today*, p. 846.
8. Samuel Escobar, "Social Concern and World Evangelism," in *Christ the Liberator*, p. 108. Excerpted from *Christ the Liberator*, compendium of the Ninth Inter-Varsity Missionary Convention. c 1971 by Inter-Varsity Christian Fellowship and used by permission of InterVarsity Press, Downers Grove, Ill.
9. *One World, One Task*, p. 43.
10. *Christianity Today*, Nov. 19, 1971, p. 188.

## CHAPTER 2

1. Robert Hall Glover, *The Progress of World-wide Missions*, p. 83. Used by permission of Harper & Row, Publishers, Inc.
2. Ibid., p. 101.
3. Edward R. Dayton, *Missions Handbook: North American Protestant Ministries Overseas*, p. 80. Used by permission.
4. Ibid., p. 91.
5. Ibid., p. 87.
6. Ibid., p. 89.
7. Ibid., pp. 421-27.
8. EFMA's official tabulation for the end of 1972 shows a total of 7,860 missionaries. This includes some 600 who are not North Americans. The remaining difference is accounted for by a slight difference in the method used in MARC's tabulation.

9. IFMA's official tabulation for the period shows 8,360 missionaries, including 1,910 who are not North Americans. The remaining difference is accounted for by a slight difference in the method used in MARC's tabulation.
10. Dayton, *Missions Handbook,* p. 86.
11. Ibid., p. 84.
12. Kenneth Scott Latourette, *Advance Through Storm,* p. 524. Used by permission of Harper & Row, Publishers, Inc.
13. W. R. Read et al., *Latin American Church Growth,* p. 51.

CHAPTER 3

1. Donald N. Larson, "Cultural Static and Religious Communication," *Evangelical Missions Quarterly* 3, no. 1 (Fall 1966):38. Used by permission.
2. Ibid., p. 42.
3. Robert C. Gordon, "The Silent Language Every Missionary Must Learn," *Evangelical Missions Quarterly* 9, no. 4 (Summer 1973):230.
4. Paul Finkenbinder, "An Open Letter," *Religious Broadcasting,* Fall 1973, p. 22.
5. Robert D. Kellum, "The Lesser Bark," *International Christian Broadcasters Bulletin,* April 1972, p. 7. Used by permission.
6. James F. Engel, "Christian Communications: Means to an End," *Asian Pulse* 4, no. 2 (June 1973):3. Used by permission.
7. Ibid.
8. Ibid., p. 5.
9. Abe Thiessen, "Matched to the Mission," *International Christian Broadcasters Bulletin,* December 1971, p. 13. Used by permission.

CHAPTER 4

1. Edward R. Dayton, *God's Purpose/Man's Plans,* p. 2. Used by permission. Mr. Dayton is director of the Missions Advanced Research and Communication Center (MARC), Monrovia, Calif.
2. Ibid., p. 15.
3. *Continuing Evangelism in Brazil,* p. 94. Used by permission.
4. Ibid., p. 95.
5. William R. Read and Frank A. Ineson, *Brazil 1980: The Protestant Handbook,* p. xxvii. Used by permission.
6. Ibid., p. 2.
7. Ibid., p. 248.
8. James Engel, "Christian Communication: Means to an End," *Asian Pulse* 4, no. 2:4. Used by permission.
9. Gordon MacDonald, "What Mission Strategy Is and Does," *Evangelical Missions Quarterly* 8, no. 1:1.
10. Ibid., p. 4.
11. *Latin America Pulse* 5, no. 5:3.

CHAPTER 5

1. Donald A. McGavran, *How Churches Grow,* p. 79. Copyright 1966, Friendship Press, New York. Used by permission.
2. Donald A. McGavran, *Bridges of God,* p. 113. Copyright 1955, Friendship Press, New York. Used by permission.
3. John T. Seamands, "What McGavran's Church Growth Thesis Means," *Evangelical Missions Quarterly* 3, no. 1:21.

4. Donald A. McGavran, *Understanding Church Growth*, p. 140. Used by permission.
5. Ibid., p. 141.
6. Seamands, p. 26.
7. C. Rene Padilla, "A Steep Climb Ahead for Theology in Latin America," *Evangelical Missions Quarterly* 7, no. 2:102.
8. Wayne Weld, "Evangelism/Church Growth Workshop in Colombia" (mimeographed report).

## CHAPTER 6

1. As quoted by Ruben Lores, "Mobilization of Believers and Churches for Evangelism," in *Mobilizing for Saturation Evangelism*, pp. 47-48.
2. Saturation Evangelism Consultation, August 1969, Leysin, Switzerland.
3. Lores, p. 48.
4. As quoted by Eileen Lageer, *New Life for All*, pp. 11-12. Used by permission.
5. Ibid., p. 68.
6. W. Dayton Roberts, *Revolution in Evangelism*, p. 112. Used by permission of Moody Press.
7. Ibid., p. 113.
8. George W. Peters, *Saturation Evangelism*, p. 127. Copyright © 1970 by Zondervan Publishing House and is used by permission.
9. Ibid., p. 72.
10. Ibid., p. 73.
11. Ibid., p. 74.
12. Ibid.
13. Ibid., p. 85.
14. Edward F. Murphy, "Follow Through Evangelism in Latin America," in *Mobilizing for Saturation Evangelism*, p. 150.
15. Ibid., p. 163.
16. Gerald O. Swank, "Building Evangelism into the Life of the Church," in *Mobilizing for Saturation Evangelism*, p. 214.

## CHAPTER 7

1. Ralph D. Winter, "This Seminary Goes to the Student," in *Theological Education by Extension*, p. 83. Used by permission of William Carey Library.
2. Ralph R. Covell and C. Peter Wagner, *An Extension Seminary Primer*, p. 6. Used by permission of William Carey Library.
3. Ibid., p. 7.
4. Peter Savage, "A Bold Move for More Realistic Theological Training," *Evangelical Missions Quarterly* 5, no. 2 (1969):66.
5. "A Different Type of College," *U. S. News and World Report*, October 4, 1971, p. 40. A copyrighted article, used by permission.
6. Ted Ward, "Programmed Learning Techniques," in *Theological Education by Extension*, ed. Ralph Winter, p. 315. Used by permission of William Carey Library.
7. Ibid., p. 327.
8. Covell and Wagner, pp. 30-31.
9. Raymond Buker, an unpublished CAMEO report to the EFMA, May 1973.

## Chapter 8

1. George W. Peters, *Saturation Evangelism*, p. 139.
2. Dennis E. Clark, *The Third World and Mission*, p. 38. Used by permission of Word Books.
3. Emerito Nacpil, "Missions But Not Missionaries," *International Review of Missions* 60, no. 239:358. Used by permission.
4. Ibid., p. 359.
5. Ibid., p. 361.
6. Kerry Lovering, "Victims of Our Own Success," *Africa Now*, Sept.-Oct. 1971, p. 2.
7. Ibid.
8. Louis L. King, "Mission/Church Relations Overseas, Part I, In Principle," in *Missions in Creative Tension*, ed. Vergil Gerber, p. 173. Used by permission of William Carey Library.
9. Ibid., p. 185.
10. George W. Peters, "Mission/Church Relations Overseas," in *Missions in Creative Tension*, ed. Vergil Gerber, p. 224. Used by permission of William Carey Library.

## Chapter 9

1. Edward R. Dayton, *Mission Handbook: North American Protestant Ministries Overseas*.
2. Evangelical Foreign Missions Association, 1405 G Street, N.W., Washington, D. C. 20005; Interdenominational Foreign Mission Association, P. O. Box 395, Wheaton, Ill. 60187; Fellowship of Missions, P. O. Box 188, Johnson City, N.Y. 13790.

## Chapter 10

1. Eric Fife, "Are Faith Missions Still on Course?" *Eternity*, Feb. 1972, p. 28. Used by permission.
2. Ibid.
3. Ibid.
4. Ibid., p. 29.

## Chapter 11

1. *One World, One Task*, p. 141.
2. Lud Golz, an unpublished statement.
3. *One World, One Task*, p. 152.
4. Ibid., p. 140.
5. *How to Organize the Mission Program in Your Church* (Jenkintown, Pa.: Neibauer, 1973).
6. Evangelical Missions Information Service, P. O. Box 794, Wheaton, Illinois 60187, the information arm of the IFMA and the EFMA.

## Chapter 12

1. *Report of the Fifth Asia Conference*, p. 193.
2. Ibid., p. 194.
3. Ibid., p. 198.
4. Ibid., p. 199.
5. Ibid.
6. James Wong et al., *Missions from the Third World*, p. 31. Used by permission.

7. *Retreat Report, 1965,* pp. 20-21.
8. James Wong, p. 131.
9. Ibid., p. 17.

## CHAPTER 13

1. *Christianity Today* 16, no. 4 (November 19, 1971):188. Quoted from Christianity Today by permission.
2. Louis L. King, "Mission/Church Relationships Overseas, Part I, In Principle," in *Missions in Creative Tension,* ed. Vergil Gerber, p. 157.
3. Dennis E. Clark, *The Third World and Mission,* p. 58.
4. Ibid., p. 59.
5. Michael Griffiths, *Give Up Your Small Ambitions,* p. 37. Used by permission.
6. Virgil R. Newbrander, An unpublished report to the Personnel and Student Affairs Committee of the IFMA and EFMA, p. 2.
7. Ibid., p. 3.
8. Intercristo, P. O. Box 9323, Seattle, Wash. 98109; Short Terms Abroad, P. O. Box 575, Downers Grove, Ill. 60515; Christian Service Corps, 1509 16th Street, N.W., Washington, D. C. 20036.

# BIBLIOGRAPHY

*Christianity Today,* Nov. 19, 1971.

Clark, Dennis E. *The Third World and Mission.* Waco, Tex.: Word, 1971.

*Continuing Evangelism in Brazil.* Monrovia, Calif.: MARC, 1971.

Covell, Ralph R., and Wagner, Peter. *An Extension Seminary Primer.* S. Pasadena, Calif.: Wm. Carey Lib., 1971.

Dayton, Edward R. *God's Purpose/Man's Plans.* Monrovia, Calif.: MARC, 1971.

———. *Mission Handbook: North American Protestant Ministries Overseas.* Monrovia, Calif.: MARC, 1973.

Engel, James. "Christian Communications: Means to an End." *Asian Pulse* 4, no. 2 (1973).

Escobar, Samuel. "Social Concern and World Evangelism." In *Christ the Liberator.* Downers Grove, Ill.: Inter-Varsity, 1971.

Fife, Eric. "Are Faith Missions Still on Course?" *Eternity.* Feb. 1972.

Finkenbinder, Paul. "An Open Letter." *Religious Broadcasting.* Fall 1973.

Gerber, Vergil, ed. *A Manual for Evangelism/Church Growth.* S. Pasadena, Calif.: Wm. Carey Lib., 1973.

———. *Missions in Creative Tension.* S. Pasadena, Calif.: Wm. Carey Lib., 1971.

Glover, Robert Hall. *The Progress of World-wide Missions.* New York: Harper & Bros., 1939.

Griffiths, Michael. *Give Up Your Small Ambitions.* London: IVP, 1970.

Hall, Clarence. "Which Way the World Council of Churches?" *Reader's Digest,* November 1971.

Kellum, Robert D. "The Lesser Bark." *International Christian Broadcasters Bulletin,* April 1972.

Lageer, Eileen. *New Life for All.* Chicago: Moody, 1970.

Larson, Donald N. "Cultural Static and Religious Communication." *Evangelical Missions Quarterly* 2, no. 1 (Fall 1966).

*Latin America Pulse* 5, no. 5.

Latourette, Kenneth Scott. *Advance Through Storm.* Grand Rapids: Zondervan, 1970.

Lores, Ruben. "Mobilization of Believers and Churches for Evangelism." In *Mobilizing for Saturation Evangelism,* ed. Clyde W. Taylor and Wade T. Coggins. Wheaton, Ill.: EMIS, 1970.

Lovering, Kerry. "Victims of Our Own Success." *Africa Now,* Sept.-Oct. 1971.

MacDonald, Gordon. "What Mission Strategy Is and Does." *Evangelical Missions Quarterly* 8, no. 1 (1971).

McGavran, Donald A. *Bridges of God.* New York: Friendship, 1955.

———. *How Churches Grow.* New York: Friendship, 1959.

———. *Understanding Church Growth.* Grand Rapids: Eerdmans, 1969.

———. "Will Uppsala Betray the Two Billion?" *Church Growth Bulletin* 4, no. 5 (May 1968).

Mosley, J. Brooke. *Christians in the Technical and Social Revolution of Our Time.* Cincinnati: Forward Movement Pubns., 1966.

Murphy, Edward F. "Follow Through Evangelism in Latin America." In *Mobilizing for Saturation Evangelism,* ed. Clyde W. Taylor and Wade T. Coggins. Wheaton, Ill.: EMIS, 1970.

Nacpil, Emerito. "Missions But Not Missionaries." *International Review of Missions* 60, no. 239 (July, 1971).

*One World, One Task.* London: Scripture Union, 1971.

Padilla, C. Rene. "A Steep Climb Ahead for Theology in Latin America." *Evangelical Missions Quarterly* 7, no. 2.

Peters, George W. *Saturation Evangelism.* Grand Rapids: Zondervan, 1970.

Read, W. R., et al. *Latin American Church Growth.* Grand Rapids: Eerdmans, 1969.

Read, William R., and Ineson, Frank A. *Brazil 1980: The Protestant Handbook.* Monrovia, Calif.: MARC, 1973.

*Report of the Fifth Asia Conference.* New York: C&MA, 1969.

*Retreat Report 1965.* Washington, D. C.: EFMA, 1965.

Roberts, W. Dayton. *Revolution in Evangelism.* Chicago: Moody, 1967.

Savage, Peter. "A Bold Move for More Realistic Theological Training." *Evangelical Missions Quarterly* 5, no. 2 (1969).

Seamands, John T. "What McGavran's Church Thesis Means." *Evangelical Missions Quarterly* 3, no. 1.

Swank, Gerald O. "Building Evangelism into the Life of the Church." In *Mobilizing for Saturation Evangelism,* ed. Clyde W. Taylor and Wade T. Coggins. Wheaton, Ill.: EMIS, 1970.

Taylor, Clyde W., and Coggins, Wade T., eds. *Mobilizing for Saturation Evangelism.* Wheaton, Ill.: EMIS, 1970.

Thiessen, Abe. "Matched to the Mission." *International Christian Broadcasters Bulletin,* December 1971.

*U. S. News and World Report,* Oct. 4, 1971.

Weld, Wayne. "Evangelism/Church Growth Workshop in Colombia." Mimeographed report circulated by the Evangelical Committee on Latin America.

Winter, Ralph, ed. *Theological Education by Extension.* S. Pasadena, Calif.: Wm. Carey Lib., 1969.

Wong, James, et al. *Missions from the Third World.* Singapore: Church Growth Center, 1973.

8 - 3 00